TIME FOR THOUGHTFULNESS

TIME FOR THOUGHTFULNESS

*A Daily Guide to Filling the World
with Love, Care and Compassion*

Ruth Fishel

Illustrations by Bonny Van de Kamp

Health Communications, Inc.®
Deerfield Beach, Florida

Publisher: **Health Communications, Inc.**
3201 S.W. 15th Street
Deerfield Beach, Florida 33442-8190

R-10-03

Cover Design by Andrea Perrine Brower

This book is dedicated to the very special people who are making a difference in the world today: the people who pray and meditate, help out in floods and earthquakes and wars, the people who do all the other work that takes so much time and energy, that requires self-transcendence. It is dedicated to the people who consciously choose for good and love, the people who are increasing the healing and loving energy of our planet and the people on it.

ACKNOWLEDGMENTS

This book would not have been possible without the help, suggestions, inspirations and knowledge of so many people. First and foremost my deepest appreciation goes to my partner, Sandy Bierig, who was up with her editing, contributions and suggestions many a morning at 5 AM before going to her "real job." It is always a joy to work with the very gifted artist Bonny Van de Kamp. I am very grateful to the people at Health Communications; publisher Peter Vegso, for having enough faith in me to offer me the opportunity to write this challenging and exciting book; editor Christine Belleris for her great ideas, enthusiasm and support; and artist Andrea Perrine Brower for her wonderful creativity and imagination.

For all the love, contributions, support and suggestions I received during the writing of this book I thank: my wonderful kids, Debbie and Richie Boisseau and Judy Fishel, the 7:30 AM Hour of Power Group, Marie Vulleumier and the other terrific people in my Cape Cod Writer's Group, Dorna Allen, Sally Butler, Diane and Donald Crosby, Andrea Lamb, Gloria Lewis, Joy Miller, Cathy Moulton, Diana Smith, Marie Stilkind, Barbara Thomas and all the special women in the Outliers, my extraordinary spiritual support group.

To the goldfinches, house finches, chickadees, nuthatches and occasional cardinals and flickers who fed at my window and gave me such beautiful moments of joy, breaking the intensity of writing this book to meet its deadline.

INTRODUCTION

Is there a God? Does God hear my prayers? If there is a God, is He or She a loving God? And if there is a loving God, why is there so much suffering? How did the world begin? Is there a reason and purpose for my life? Why am I here?

Or is there just energy, a force, a spirit. . . something "out there" that makes everything happen? Can I tap that energy? Am I part of that energy? Or is it an aimless, purposeless random accident, a result of gases and chemicals coming together to form the beginning of what we now call life.

Human beings have asked these questions for as long as we have had the capacity to think and reason. Some people claim to have the answers. Many follow those who say they know the answers. Wise teachers, such as Moses, Christ, the Buddha, Lao Tze, teach a path to follow. The wisest of all the teachers tell us there is no "right way," that each of us have to find "our own way."

Years ago I was guided to a quote by Erich Fromme who wrote that God is infinite. Man is finite. Therefore we cannot define God. All I know today is that there is a Power greater than me, a force, an energy in the universe. I, personally, do not have absolute answers, but I have discovered "my way." I have found my path to a Higher Power. I practice prayer and meditation daily to connect with my purpose and my strength to accomplish this purpose. Over the years I have come to know what is right for me by how I feel and by observing the results of my actions.

Whether you are a believer or disbeliever, a follower, a leader or a loner, matters not right now. What matters is that the world and the people in it are in trouble and this book will raise your awareness and, ultimately, the awareness of more and more people.

Here is what I do know. Thought is energy. Thought creates words. Words are energy. Words connect people. Words have power. Words that result in actions have greater power.

Loving thoughts make me feel loving. Angry thoughts make me feel angry. If I feel loving, I can be giving to myself and others. If I am angry, I can act out my anger toward myself and others.

My mood can affect the people I meet. My energy extends from my body.

When I take time to be thoughtful, I enter into a deeper connection with my inner spirit. I reach a greater awareness of my connection with everything in the universe. I feel one with all beings.

When I take time to be thoughtful, I am connected with everyone reading these words. I am connected with all of you concerned with the violence and pain and suffering that is in our world today.

Scientists tell us there is something called critical mass. If enough people think or pray the same thoughts at the same time, things change. Most of us today are aware that if the world is to change, we need to change.

The world can be uplifted by the power of our thoughts, our actions and our words. For example, if a large number of people share the same thoughts each day, it will help us in reaching that critical mass which can lift up the world's thinking and change it for good.

Time for Thoughtfulness is a daily guide with a weekly format. Each week consists of inspirational quotes, suggestions to think about and suggestions for actions we can take for ourselves and others. As more and more of us bring our thoughtful attention to the fundamental principles of goodness and love, the world changes.

If a particular idea or suggestion does not feel appropriate for you, just skip to another page. You can read it a page at a time or at random.

The world mirrors what we think and thus what we feel. If we feel hostile, we will be living in a hostile world. If we feel loving, the world will show us how loving it is.

The important thing to know is that we can make a difference, that we are making a difference. We need to give ourselves a big PAT ON THE BACK, knowing we are doing God's work, the heart work.

God bless you all for being here and sharing the heart work.

With love, peace and light,
Ruth

Thoughtfulness is an energy, a powerful, positive and loving energy. Thoughtfulness is so powerful it can help another person feel soft and warm. Thoughtfulness has the power to melt a cold heart, put an end to resentments and open the way to trust.

Thoughtfulness takes practice.
Today is a perfect day to begin.

Today's Thoughtful
Action Step/Touching Someone

A thoughtful touch can bring tears of joy or it can release tears of pain. A touch can let you know you are not alone. Thoughtfulness can heal.

Today I will touch someone with love through my words, actions or thoughts.

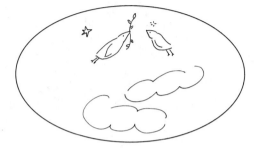

Affirmation/Giving

It feels so good to know I have something to give to someone else today! Even if it is only a smile or a loving thought, I know there is always something that I have that can make someone else feel better.

Today I will take time to reflect on
what the following thought means to me:

Thought is the strongest thing we have.
Work done by true and profound thought,
that is real force.

—Albert Schweitzer

When I take the time to be thoughtful, I know just what to do when the time is right. I no longer have to struggle for my answers. I come to a deeper respect for my connection to what is appropriate in the moment.

As I learn more and more to come from my true self, I grow in the ability to trust my impulses and act on them.

Today's Thoughtful Action
Step/Community

Today I will increase my thoughtfulness in my community, being more mindful of including rather than excluding others. I'll look for ways to open my life and let more people into it. If I can bring more people into a project or ask the opinions of others before I make a decision, I will.

If I can take part of the credit and give the other part to someone else, I will.

I will be more aware of the energy given and received when I am coming from this place of community.

I will observe how I feel when I do this and how I perceive my actions are being received.

**Today I will take time to rest
and review my week.**

Where have I been thoughtful?

Can I see results from my thoughtfulness?

Am I aware of any thoughtful actions
by other people to me this week?

How do I feel about myself as a result
of my thoughtfulness?

What did I learn this week?

Can I see that I am making a difference in the world?

It's important to feel good about
myself today and acknowledge myself for
my actions and thoughts, as well as my
intentions!

I must remember that I am on a path
of progress, not perfection!

One thing I know: the only ones
among you who will be really happy
are those who will have
sought and found how to serve.

— Albert Schweitzer

The more we struggle to seek happiness by acquiring money or possessions, the farther away we are from living a satisfied life. There will always be a faint feeling inside that something is missing. We can spend our entire lives acquiring material things, yet this feeling will never go away.

When we spend a portion of our lives helping people who cannot do for themselves, we will come to the big "AHA!" and feelings of warmth and love will erase that empty feeling. Personal satisfaction will light our path.

Today's Thoughtful Action
Step/At Least One Smile

As I go about my day today, I will wait for the right moment and trust that I will know who can benefit from my smile. This does not have to be a logical, well-analyzed action. I'll simply trust my inner guidance and smile when it feels right. We will both feel warmer as a result.

Affirmation/Thoughts and Feelings

It has been proven that the words we think are so powerful, they can actually change the chemicals in our brain, affecting how we feel.

Today I will bring my awareness to my own thoughts, knowing that I am responsible for the way I feel in each given moment.

Today I will watch my thoughts closely, noticing the relationship between them and how I feel emotionally, physically and spiritually. Today will be a learning, practicing, experiencing day. I will enjoy my findings rather than judge them!

Today I will take time to reflect on what the following thought means to me:

Thought is cause:
experience is effect.
If you don't like the effects
in your life,
you have to change the nature
of your thinking.

—Marianne Williamson
A Return To Love

When I take the time to be thoughtful, I enter into a deeper connection with my inner spirit. I reach a greater awareness to my connection with everything in the universe. I feel one with all beings. I know I am not alone.

Today's Thoughtful Action
Step/Gratitude List

A gratitude list is a wonderful way to bring attention to the good in our lives. So often we get caught up in our wants and desires, forgetting to value what we have.

It's so easy to slip into wishful thinking, hoping that things will be different, waiting for something to happen or wanting someone to change. This kind of thinking keeps us from being alive in the present moment.

Today I will keep my focus on the now, finding the good things in my life and writing them down on my gratitude list.

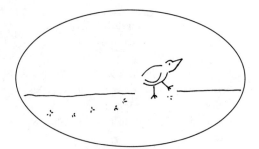

**Today I will take time
to rest and review my week.**

Where have I been thoughtful this
week?

Can I see positive results from my
action steps?

14

Recently I sat with a friend who has AIDS as he came to realize that living meant something good to him, at last. At the same time he knew that he was really dying. He talked and I listened, not trying to fix anything, knowing I couldn't. We both cried and when he was finished expressing his grief I hugged him tightly. I was so grateful that I was able to be thoughtful and just listen.

—Sandy Bierig
Family Therapist/Author

Today's Thoughtful Action
Step/Living Eulogy

It usually takes someone's death to have anything good written about them. When someone dies, people gather together and give thought to the good that someone did in their lives. What a shame that people rarely have the opportunity to hear the good things said about them when they are alive!

Find a person you respect and admire and take some time to bring them into your thoughts. Write a living eulogy to this person. Write down everything you can think of that is positive and good about that person. Then give it to them. Let that person enjoy it now!

Affirmation/Being Considerate

The words _thoughtful_ and _considerate_ can be used synonymously. Both also take practice.

Today I will carefully bring my thoughts to new areas where I can be more considerate of others. Today I will be kind wherever and whenever possible.

Today I will take time to reflect on what the following thought means to me:

Nobody could make a greater mistake than he who did nothing because he could only do a little.

—Edmund Burke

When I take the time to be thoughtful,
I can try softer. I can let go of struggle. I
can go with the flow.

Today's Thoughtful Action
Step/Preparing for the Future

The next time I am cooking a meal, I'll make more than I need. Then I will freeze the extra portions. This will give me meals to have on hand for emergencies.

When I know that someone can be helped by having a meal brought to them, I'll have one ready in no time, and with very little effort!

I can be doing something good for others in the future and I don't even need to know who they are today!

**Today I will take time to rest and
review my week.**

Where have I been thoughtful this
week?

Can I see results from my thoughtfulness?

What did I learn this week?

Can I see that I am making a difference in the world?

When a goose gets sick or wounded
or shot down, two geese drop
out of the formation
and follow her down to help
and protect her.
They stay with her until she is either
able to fly again or dies.
Then they start out again, either
joining another formation or
catching up with the original flock.

Lesson: If we have as much sense as the geese, we'll combine our strengths and stand by each other, just as they do.

Flying in Formation (Or, We Need to
Know What the Wild Goose Knows),
—Author Unknown

Today's Thoughtful Action
Step/Easy-Does-It Giving

Being generous does not have to be a big deal! I do not have to give the shirt off my back! I do not have to give the food off my table. I need not deprive myself or my family of anything that I want or need.

A smile can be enough.

Holding the door open for someone can feel good.

I will do at least one generous thing, just one easy thing, today.

Affirmation/Natural Order

Today I am taking time to give thought to the patterns, rhythms and natural order in the universe. As I observe nature, I am relating these truths to my own life. I am finding ways to discover and honor my own inner rhythms. I am simplifying my life so that it is more open to living in the context of my purpose and connection to the universe.

Today I will take time to reflect on
what the following thought means to me:

*We must understand that
all personal growth is intended
for the awakening of the whole.*

—Richard Moss

When I take the time to be thoughtful, I know I am connected with everyone reading this book. I know I am connected to people who are deeply concerned with the violence and pain in our world today. I know I am connected with a wonderful group of people who care and are committed to making the world a better place for everyone.

This is a very powerful connection and it makes me feel strong.

Today's Thoughtful Action
Step/Generosity

Some time ago I developed a habit that has brought great pleasure. I buy a roll of nickels or dimes and leave them in a place children might find them. I toss them in the sand, in the playground or near children's books in a store. The excitement on a child's face upon finding them brings me joy. Often I keep extra quarters in my purse for check-out lines. If Mom or Dad says it's okay, I love to give a quarter to a child for a treat. (No parent has ever declined.) It costs so little to bring delight, surprise and happiness to a child.

—Sharon Wegscheider-Cruse
Family Therapist/Author

Today I will take time to rest and review my week.

Did I have a gut feeling or thought to call or visit someone this week and not do it?

Was I too busy?

I can follow through with one action that I did not take this week and enjoy the good feelings I get in return.

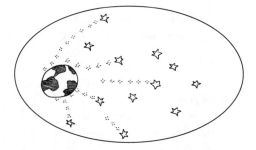

Thoughtfulness is. . . inclusive, community. honoring differences, familial, being thoughtful about one's own assumptions, especially surrounding invisible disabilities. It's looking for opportunities to listen. Awareness and acceptance. And by understanding each other's differences, we can make peace.

—Brainstorming "thoughtfulness" at a Women's Passover Seder, Cape Cod

Today's Thoughtful Action
Step/Exercise Your Mind

I am becoming more and more aware that my mind and spirit need exercise as well as my body. Through prayer, meditation, physical exercise, reading and thoughtful actions, I am developing a personal program for physical, mental and spiritual growth. My intention is to make it a program I can fit into my life and follow daily.

Affirmation/Practicing Positive Thinking

As a verb the word _thought_ means:

_The act or process of using the mind actively and
deliberately; meditation; cogitation._

—Funk and Wagnalls
Standard College Dictionary

Today I am learning that with practice
I can direct my thinking. More and more
I am learning to direct my thinking to
thoughts of love, kindness and forgiveness. I am learning to let go of thoughts
that come from fear, anger and resentments. Practicing a day at a time, I am
using my thinking ability to improve the
quality of my life and the lives of those
around me.

I am deliberately bringing my attention to areas where I can change anything
negative or destructive in my life to something positive.

Today I will take time to reflect on what the following thought means to me:

If you can, help others; if you cannot do that, at least do not harm them.

—Randy Rind
quoted in *Chop Wood, Carry Water*

When I take the time to be thoughtful, I can let go of all the racing thoughts that keep me from feeling peaceful. I can let go of my worries and fears, my "shoulds" and "shouldn'ts," my criticisms and judgments.

I feel a deeper sense of peace and I can pass it on.

Today's Thoughtful Action
Step/Compliment

Even a compliment can be hard to give when we feel needy ourselves.

Today I will identify an area where I would like to be complimented and give that compliment to someone else.

**Today I will take time to rest and
review my week.**

How much have I received from
myself this week?

How much have I been willing to
reach out to others?

How much have I been willing to
learn from my own shortcomings?

I want to keep learning to give to
others.

I have choices about everything that goes on in my life today. I can keep my world very small by thinking that the problems of everyone else are far too big for me to help. I can keep my mind closed to any possibilities that I might have something to give. I can remain detached.

Or I can go out into the world and actually meet the people who are suffering. I can open my heart to their pain and connect with it.

I can let my heart tell me what to do. I choose this path today.

**Today's Thoughtful Action
Step/Surprise**

Planning a surprise for someone lets them know how much you care. Maybe it will be just sitting quietly with them, anticipating how they may be feeling and being a friend.

—Janet Farrell

Affirmation/Love

*Someday, after we have mastered the
winds, the waves, the tides and
gravity, we shall harness for God the
energies of love. Then, for the second time
in the history of the world,
man will have discovered fire.*

—Teilhard de Chardin

Today I will experience the power of
love by giving it away!

Today I will take time to reflect on
what the following thought means to me:

Have you a kindness shown?
Pass it on;
'Twas not given for thee alone,
Pass it on;
Let it travel down the years,
Let it wipe another's tears,
'Til in Heaven the deed appears,
Pass it on.

—Henry Burtton
Pass It On

When I take the time to be thoughtful,
I can consider today's important question:
Have I learned to be more aware of when
I am burdening others with my moods?

Today's Thoughtful Action
Step/Living Eulogy

Today I will act out of my own inner vision, reaching toward a future of satisfied longings and moving away from past disappointments.

Within each day is a golden opportunity, a gift.

Today I name, cherish and accept the gifts put before me.

When I appreciate what has been given me, I act more loving and grateful toward others.

The world is in need of my vision today.

Let peace begin by having a right spirit within me.

—Anne Ierardi
Pastoral Counselor/Minister

**Today I will take time to rest and
review my week.**

How much have I received from
myself this week?

How much have I been willing to
reach out to others?

How much have I been willing to learn
from my own shortcomings?

It feels so good to acknowledge my
progress!

Six million Jews died. Millions of Vietnamese, hundreds of Chinese, thousands of Iraqis, Kuwaitis, Africans, Pakistanis, Ethiopians, children in American cities and towns. We could go on and on and on. . .

When is enough enough?!!

Today's Thoughtful Action
Step/Send Compassion

Today I will remember one person
who has had someone they love die within the past year. I will write a note or send
a card, letting that person know that I am
thinking about them. Being touched in
this way by someone who cares enough to
take this time helps make the pain of loss
easier to get through.

Affirmation/God

Today I take time to bring my thoughts to the God of my understanding, knowing this is where I receive my guidance, my strength and my peace.

Today I will take time to reflect on what the following thought means to me:

Lord, make me an instrument of your peace.
Where there is hatred, let me sow love,
Where there is injury, pardon,
Where there is doubt, faith,
Where there is despair, hope,
Where there is darkness, light,
And where there is sadness, joy.

O, Divine Master, grant that
I may not so much seek to be consoled,
as to console;
To be understood, as to understand;
To be loved, as to love;
For it is in giving that we receive,
It is in pardoning that we are pardoned;
And it is in dying that we are
born to eternal life.

—St. Francis of Assisi

When I take the time to be thoughtful, I know just what to do for others when the time is right.

Today's Thoughtful Action
Step/Practice Giving

Today's action step is to merely give something to someone. There is no right or wrong here. Simply give whatever feels right at the moment.

Bring your awareness to the people you come in contact with today. Be open to where you can do the most good. Be ready and you will find the right opportunities to give.

Be aware of how it makes you feel.

Then smile and give yourself a secret little pat on the back!

Today I will take time to rest and review my week.

Am I growing in my awareness of ways to be thoughtful?

Am I practicing these new ways?

Am I turning negative thoughts to positive ones?

Am I being loving to myself and others?

Today I will remember to say *I love you* to everyone that is important in my life!

One evening two women were walking along the beach. Lying on the sand at the water's edge were hundreds of starfish. One of the women bent down and began throwing the starfish back in the ocean. The other woman said, "You are wasting your time. You can never save them all."

The first woman continued throwing the starfish into the ocean, one at a time.

"No," she said. "But I can save this one. And this one. And this one."

Today's Thoughtful Action
Step/Attention

Today I will give my full attention to each person I meet. I will stop all I am doing and truly listen to them with my ears, eyes and heart fully open.

—Leslie Sjosidt

Affirmation/Courage

_Behold the turtle, who makes progress only
when she sticks out her neck._

Today I have the courage to face life as
it is and make progress a part of my life.

I am willing to take chances and grow
and risk and feel fully alive!

Today I move beyond my fear and
complacency so that I can find a way to
be thoughtful. I know I will feel much
better about myself and will be making
someone else feel better with my progress!

Today I will take time to reflect on what the following thought means to me:

*If we don't like the world we're in,
there is always the option
to create the world we desire with
our acts of kindness.*

—Hanoch and Meladee McCarty
Acts of Kindness

When I take the time to be thoughtful, I can let myself be who I am. I can also let others be who they are. I can let the world be what it is. I can simply be me!

Today's Thoughtful Action
Step/Healing a Relationship

Think about a relationship you would like to heal. Take some time to be alone where you can be thoughtful. Bring your awareness to the relationship that you have chosen. Let yourself be open to anything good and positive about this relationship. Write your thoughts down.

When you are ready, you can share these thoughts. You don't have to do this today if you choose not to! Being willing to take the time to heal this relationship is enough for today!

Healing begins with willingness.

**Today I will take time to rest and
review my week.**

I want to keep learning to give to
others.

Have I taken enough time to be
thoughtful to myself this week?

I must continue to remind myself that
if I am not thoughtful to myself, I have
nothing to give anyone else.

Am I listening to the people who need
to be heard?

*Some people come into our lives and quickly go. . .
Some people stay for a while and leave their
footprints on our hearts, and we are never,
ever the same.*

—Flavia

Looking back over the friends I have had in my life, I remember with warm feelings the ones who were always there for me. In times of need or in times of celebration, they showed up. They participated in a way that was right for them at that moment. Some participated with a card or a phone call, others with their presence or touch. The right look or word has made a painful time easier to bear.

I remember those moments with deep gratitude.

Today I will look for opportunities to be like those friends who have stayed in my heart.

Today's Thoughtful Action Step/Simplify

Today I am bringing my attention to all the things I do in my life. I will discover one area, no matter how small, that I can give up to make my life lighter and easier.

This will reduce my stress and leave more time for the important things in my life and the world.

Affirmation/Suggestions

There comes a time when the most thoughtful thing one can do for another is to let go. We can encourage, support, advise and suggest. Once this is done, we must let go of the results. Each person must learn their own lessons and follow their own path. God's will for us is not necessarily the same as God's will for someone else.

Today I will pay attention to the suggestions I offer, knowing they are merely my thoughts, not laws or rules.

Leap Year Reflection.

Today I will take time to reflect on what the following thought means to me:

. . . it is through giving that we receive . . .

—St. Francis of Assisi

Today I will take time to reflect on what the following thought means to me:

The more I work with people and the more I go through life, the more I realize that people just want to be happy. If I take five minutes out of each day to remember to treat people the same way I want to be treated, we could accomplish wonderful things together.

—Bob Fishel (1963-1992)
Five Minutes for World Peace

When I take the time to be thoughtful, I feel the excitement of knowing I am part of a movement that is helping to make the world a better place to live.

**Today's Thoughtful Action
Step/Taking Time**

Today I am taking time to stop and smell the flowers.

**Today I will take time to rest and
review my week.**

Where did I take my own needs too
lightly?

Where did I put others before me in
ways that did me harm?

Am I becoming more gentle and less
demanding of myself?

Am I taking time to take care of me?

Am I expecting too much from
myself?

Can I love and value myself today?

As more and more of us further develop our ability to be thoughtful, we will see that thoughtfulness has the power to heal the world.

Today's Thoughtful Action Step/Simplify

Today, with thoughtfulness, I will examine all my mail. What can I give up to make my life more simple and give me more space both mentally and physically? What I can let go of to reduce the clutter in my life?

Can I write to have junk mail stopped? Are there catalogues or brochures that I can choose not to receive?

Today I will eliminate at least one piece of regular mail that comes into my life. I will be thoughtful not only to myself but to the entire planet.

Affirmation/Connecting with Others

Today I feel the power of my spiritual connection to all the people who are thoughtfully changing their attitudes and thus changing the world.

Today I will take time to reflect on what the
following thought means to me:

*Insight is of no use unless it results
in action. From our deep awareness
of our shared desire to avoid pain
comes a sense of responsibility
to relieve others of suffering.*

—The Dalai Lama

When I take the time to be thoughtful, I can consider today's important question:

What can I do today to offer hope to young people?

So much of the violence in our society is caused by the hopelessness young people feel. They see no hope in their future. I can join together with others who are finding ways to encourage and support young children. Today I will begin to explore where I can be a positive influence in our society.

Today's Thoughtful Action Step/Friendship

*A friend may well be reckoned
the masterpiece of nature.*

—Ralph Waldo Emerson

What a wonderful, warm feeling it gives me to think of telling one of my friends that he or she reminds me of this quote today. I can't wait to do it!

**Today I will take time to rest
and review my week.**

Am I giving freely to others in ways
that really matter?

Am I learning to let go of what I no
longer need and recycle where they will
do more good?

Where have I been thoughtful?

Have I been allowing myself to feel
the pleasure in giving?

Thoughtfulness begins within us. Gestures of thoughtfulness are as simple as a smile, a nod or eye contact with a passerby. Sharing ourselves in this way sends a message that we care. And it gives us the opportunity to greet each person with respect and kindness and open our heart to loving ways.

—Joy Miller
Therapist/Author

Today's Thoughtful Action Step/Change

Today I will be conscious of a change I can make in someone else's life. They might not know what I did or that I did it, but I will do something that will make a difference for someone else.

Affirmation/Closer to God

*Today I will take time to be thoughtful of me,
so that I will become more in touch
with my higher self.
When I am closer to my higher self,
I am closer to others.*

—Anne N. Harmon

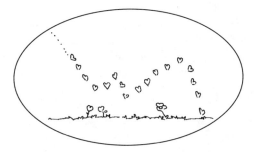

Today I will take time to reflect on what the following thought means to me:

The perfume of sandalwood,
the scent of rosebay and jasmine,
travel only as far as the wind.
But the fragrance of goodness travels
with us through all the worlds.
Like the garlands woven
from a heap of flowers, fashion your life
as a garland of beautiful deeds.

—The Buddha

When I take the time to be thoughtful, I can consider today's important question: In every neighborhood there is an infirm or elderly person who could use my help one day a month or so. If they had this help, perhaps they could stretch out the time when they could stay and enjoy living in their own homes. Can I donate some of my time in this way? If I can't do this, what can I do?

But when we make an effort to move ourselves away from self and begin to concentrate on the needs of others and how to serve them, we begin to heal. Service is balm to both the spirit and body.

—Betty Eadie

Today's Thoughtful Action
Step/Spread the Word

When enough of us are aware of something, all of us
become aware of it.

—Ken Keyes, Jr.
The Hundredth Monkey

Today I will make at least one other
person aware of the power of our
thoughts and the need to spread that
power in the form of loving thoughts to
all people on this planet.

**Today I will take time to rest and
review my week.**

Am I valuing the goodness in myself
and sharing it freely?

Am I caring for myself as well as for
others?

--- --- ---

--- --- ---

--- --- ---

--- --- ---

--- --- ---

Sometimes we are so caught up with our own needs that we become insensitive to the needs of others. We might even take our moods and frustrations out on others.

As we grow in awareness, we learn to stop and think before we act. We learn to be in charge of our actions and choose to be good and kind, even when we don't want to do so.

Today's Thoughtful Action
Step/Following Through

Our words, our actions, must consciously set the stage
for the life we wish to live.

—Marlo Morgan
Mutant Message Down Under

Good intentions just aren't enough. We must actively participate in creating a positive and healthy way of life for ourselves and those around us.

I will watch for ways to do this today.

Affirmation/Daily Plan

I will be thoughtful about my day today. To have the kind of day I deserve, I will put thought into my daily plan. In that way, my day will be well thought-out, placing first things first, setting limits, acknowledging what I can do.

Peace of mind and serenity are the results of being thoughtful about my day, so that I can be thoughtful, caring, kind and considerate of those around me.

—Pam Boden

Today I will take time to reflect on what the following thought means to me:

I am of the opinion that my life belongs
to the whole community and, as long as I live,
it is my privilege to do for it whatever I can.
I want to be thoroughly used up when I die.
For the harder I work, the more I live.
I rejoice my life for its own sake.
Life is no brief candle to me.
It is a sort of splendid torch which
I've got to hold up for the moment and
I want to make it burn as brightly
as possible before handing it over
to future generations.

—George Bernard Shaw
(as quoted by Steven Covey)

When I take the time to be thoughtful, I bring more awareness to my life. I notice my upsets. I am aware when I feel agitated. I bring my attention to everything I feel, whether pleasant or unpleasant. I don't have to push any feelings away.

If I resist unpleasant feelings, I will stay upset and separated from those around me. I won't think that I have to look for an escape from those feelings. Whatever I feel, I know that it is okay.

If I am open to all I feel and accept it, my mind will not be busy judging my feelings and I can be open to the moment, the experience and the people in it.

Today's Thoughful Action Step/Comfort

Today I am giving love and comfort to someone who needs help during a difficult time.

The source of love is deep in us, and
we can help others realize a lot of happiness.
One word, one action, one thought
can reduce another person's suffering
and bring that person joy.

—Thich Nhat Hanh

**Today I will take time to rest and
review my week.**

I know that a thought is just that until
I act on it. Making a decision and putting
it into effect is what action is all about.

Am I moving past intention into action
today?

Did I stop to be aware of the needs of
others in my life this week?

Did I place first things first?

> *Let it be done unto me*
> *according to your word.*
>
> —Mary, mother of Jesus

Discerning God's will for me and following it can sometimes be a very fearful prospect. What if I am asked to do something I don't want to do?! What if I can't?! But, through my experience I've come to know that living God's will is my purpose and ultimate joy.

I pray in faith today for the grace to empower me to carry it through.

—Megan Pettit

Today's Thoughtful Action
Step/Affirm Someone Terrific!

The world is full of so many terrific human beings. Our attention is usually focused on the other people who are doing damage or on all the things we are not doing. It is imperative that we take time to acknowledge the good that is being done in this world by so many.

Today I will affirm at least one other human being. I will acknowledge his or her contribution to our planet.

Affirmation/Make a Difference

Today I can find one thing to do that will make a difference in at least one person's life. No act is too small to make a difference.

Today I will take time to reflect on
what the following thought means to me:

*When we're working solely for money,
our motivation is getting rather than giving.
The miraculous transformation here is
a shift from a sales mentality
to a service mentality.*

A Course in Miracles

When we take the time to be thoughtful, we grow. We change. Our own under-standing of spirituality changes. It may broaden, deepen or shift. It may become confused or feel as if it has disappeared completely. But it does not stay still. As long as we pray and meditate, our knowl-edge of God and our relationship to God continues to grow.

We can never say our way is _the way_ because our way is only what it is, in each moment. When appropriate, we can share our journey, relating where we began, what we have experienced along the way, and where we are now. Others can listen and benefit from whatever they choose. With willingness, each one of us will find our own way.

Today's Thoughtful Action Step/Action

Today I will turn at least one good thought into one good action.

**Today I will take time to rest and
review my week.**

Have I prayed this week for the power
I need to do my work?

Have I affirmed my awareness of others in the world who are making contributions to its well-being?

Have I "stepped" outside of myself in
order to notice my own growth?

*As a bird flaps its wings, it creates an
"uplift" for the birds following.
By flying in a "V" formation, the flock's
flying range is 71 percent longer than
if each bird flew alone.*

Lesson: People who share a common
direction and sense of community can get
where they are going quicker and easier
by traveling on the thrust of one another.

*Flying in Formation (Or, We Need to
Know What the Wild Goose Knows)*
—Author Unknown

**Today's Thoughtful Action
Step/Healing a Relationship**

Today I will find a relationship that
needs mending or one that feels distant or
cold. I'll take a deep breath and give it
something to warm it up or fill a space.

Affirmation/My Day to Be Gentle

When we are coming from a place of need, it is very difficult to practice thoughtfulness. Our own pain and emptiness can overcome all thoughts of the needs of other people. Know that this is alright and natural. These are the times when we have to take care of ourselves and find thoughtful things to do for ourselves, knowing that this time will not be forever and it will pass.

Today I will take time to bring thought to all the ways that I can be gentle with myself, allowing myself to feel exactly what I feel, and affirming that I am okay.

Today I will take time to reflect on what the following thought means to me:

A loving person lives in a loving world.
A hostile person lives in a hostile world.
Everyone you meet is your mirror.

—Ken Keyes, Jr.

When I take the time to be thoughtful,
I can consider today's important question:
How can I make my home a more peace-
ful place in which to live?

**Today's Thoughtful Action
Step/Thoughtfulness to Humanity**

Today I will do something positive to express my protest against human suffering. I can write a letter, make a phone call or begin a local petition. I can tell others to do the same.

The more people who take action at the same time, the more we can change the energy of the universe and make a difference.

Today I will take time to rest and review my week.

Do I see the results of my thoughtfulness?

Have people been more thoughtful with me?

Am I attracting more positive and loving people in my life?

Am I attracted to more positive and loving people?

God has blessed each of us in different, beautiful and special ways. When we share ourselves with others, we give gifts of love, friendship and caring. In this way we help feed the hungry, clothe the naked and comfort the lonely and ill. We become friends. When we do these things, we often find we are blessed as much as, and perhaps more than, those we help.

—Shirley Pieters Vogel

Today's Thoughtful Action Step/No Action

During times of disappointment or discouragement I will seek the thoughtful thing to do. I will look for the lesson I need to learn. I will pray for the guidance to know when no action is the best action.

Affirmation/Easy Giving

The Buddha said there are three kinds of giving. One is giving what we no longer want. That is easy. Next is sharing what we have. That is harder. The third is being free and willing to give anything and everything, being attached to nothing. That is very hard!

Today I will practice easy giving, that which I can do without strain or resentment. I will develop my generosity slowly and let it come naturally.

Today I will take time to reflect on what the following thought means to me:

> *Humility is a function of*
> *how you view others.*
> *Your attention is directed outward.*
> *Arrogance is making yourself great*
> *at the expense of another;*
> *humility is realizing that,*
> *whatever your greatness, power,*
> *knowledge, grace, or even kindness,*
> *you are never greater than another.*

—Rabbi Lawrence Kushner

When I take the time to be thoughtful, I can consider today's important question: In the Judaic tradition people practice _gemilut hasidim,_ deeds of loving kindness. This would include giving things to the poor without embarrassing or degrading them so they could keep their dignity intact.

I have seen people leave piles of wood or an old piece of furniture by the side of the road with a "FREE" sign.

What can I give today and how can I give it so as not to embarrass anyone?

Today's Thoughtful Action
Step/Friendship

Today I am bringing my thoughts to a
friend I have not seen in a long time. If I
know where my friend is, I can either
write or call, letting my friend know that
he is on my mind. If I can't actually make
this physical connection, I will pass on
loving thoughts with my friend in mind.
Either way, I will be adding positive and
loving energy to the universe.

**Today I will take time to rest and
review my week.**

Did I make a commitment to an action
step and forget to do it?

Can I forgive myself and let it go?

Can I see the results from the actions
that I did accomplish?

Am I aware of any thoughtful actions
directed at me?

What did I learn this week?

Can I see that I am making a difference in the world?

We are not human beings on a spiritual path but spiritual beings on a human path!

—Jean Shinoda Bolen

As a human being, I am so complicated! I must eat, sleep and have fresh air and exercise, but my physical well-being is not enough. I must also see that I am emotionally fit by managing my stress. My spiritual health is the most important because without it I could not value myself at all.

**Today's Thoughtful Action
Step/Feeding the Hungry**

Today I will take the time to find a way that is right for me to relieve at least one person from the pains of hunger and thirst.

*My miracle is that when I feel hungry I eat,
and when I feel thirsty I drink.*

—Bankei, Zen Master

Affirmation/Closer to God

Today I will take time to be thoughtful of me, so that I will become more in touch with my higher self. When I am closer to my higher self, I am closer to others.

—Anne N. Harmon
Author

Today I will take time to reflect on
what the following thought means to me:

*In each person there is a priceless treasure
that is in no other. Therefore, one shall
honor each person for the hidden value
that only this person and
no one else has.*

—Martin Buber

When I take the time to be thoughtful,
I can consider today's important question:
What can I do today to make the world a
better place for at least one other person?

Today's Thoughtful Action
Step/Compliments

Share a compliment you might have heard about someone. The recipient will feel grand and the giver will have her gift delivered. You'll telegraph cheer from far and wide.

—Christine Belleris
Editor

**Today I will take time to rest and
review my week.**

Today I can give myself permission to
feel good about myself! Even if I didn't
do all that I thought I would do, I am now
more conscious about how I can change
my own world.

That in itself feels good!

A recent study showed that in one of two groups of heart patients, those who were prayed for did better than those for whom prayers were not said. Neither the doctors nor the patients knew which group was being prayed for, but the patients receiving prayers improved significantly. What a wonderful act of thoughtfulness for an invalid or a shut-in! And what a wonderful gift to give to others: the gift of prayer!

—Marie Stilkind
Editor

Today's Thoughtful Action
Step/Feeding the Hungry

Some supermarkets have barrels for customers to contribute cans of food for the homeless and the poor. When disasters such as floods or earthquakes occur, these contributions become earmarked for suffering people. Today I will find a market that does not have a specific area set up for this purpose. I will provide the inspiration for this idea!

Affirmation/Faithful

Today I know that being faithful to myself is the best way to keep faith with others, leaving me, in the end, without regret for my choices.

Today I will take time to reflect on
what the following thought mean to me:

*Real generosity toward the future consists
in giving all to what is present.*

—Albert Camus

When I take the time to be thoughtful, I can consider today's important question: What can I do today to help influence young people to belong to society in a healthy way?

Some young people act in a violent manner when they are not really violent people. They desperately want to belong and they will do anything to fit in.

Can I find a way to improve this situation? I can look into volunteering as a tutor or as a Big Brother or Big Sister. If these ideas are not right for me, what else can I do?

Today's Thoughtful Action
Step/Taking Time to Praise

The next time I pass a nice yard or a pretty garden, I'll take the time to let the gardener know I appreciate their work. It would really be thoughtful to let them know how much enjoyment I receive when I pass by their creations.

Today I will take time to rest and review my week.

Has my progress been for others as well as myself this week?

Have I carried out my action steps?

Do I try to live so that I will not feel regret in the future for my actions today?

Have I fostered healthy growth in the young?

A friend of mine called me and she sounded very upset. She wanted to know what a friend had said about her at a party.

"I know she said something about me. She was staring at me all evening."

"Yes. She did say something," I told her. "She said that you looked stunning."

My friend was shocked, then flustered, then delighted. She hung up the phone feeling wonderful. But how unfortunate that she felt paranoid and insecure for a whole day before we spoke.

If you are thinking a good thought about someone, say it out loud to them. Unexpressed thoughts that could make someone else feel good are wasted.

—Mary Littleford

**Today's Thoughtful Action
Step/Taking Time for Me**

Sometimes we are so busy doing for
everyone else that we forget to do for ourselves. This may take more effort but if
we give ourselves a treat, doing for others may not always feel so demanding.

*Today I will be as kind to myself as if
I am really someone else!*

—Debbie Fishel Boisseau

Affirmation/Focusing on My Soul

In my quiet time today, I will bring my full awareness to the direction my soul wants to take. If I do not find a clear action step for today, I will remain focused throughout the day, knowing that the opportunity will present itself as long as my mind remains open.

Focus is composed of sensing, hearing and following the directions of the soul-voice.

—Clarissa Pinkola Estes, Ph.D.
Women Who Run with the Wolves

Today I will take time to reflect on what the following thought means to me:

To every man there openeth
A Way and Ways, and a Way,
And the High Soul climbs the High Way,
And the low soul gropes the Low,
And in between, on the misty flats,
The rest drift to and fro.
But to every man there openeth
A High Way, and a Low,
And every man decideth
The Way his soul shall go.

—John Oxenham

When I take the time to be thoughtful,
I can consider today's important question:
Wouldn't it be wonderful to have a scholarship fund set up in memory of all children who have been killed by violence!
Wouldn't it be wonderful to offer hope to
young people, letting this scholarship
fund be the vehicle that could send them
off to higher education!

If I personally do not have the time or
ability required to organize such a fund,
what else can I do to help make it happen? One thing I can do is pass this idea
on to others. What else can I do?

Today's Thoughtful Action Step/Sharing the Importance of Thoughtful Actions

Today I will share the importance of thoughtfulness with at least one other person. This will give someone else an opportunity to add to their own good feelings as well as contributing to the healing of the planet.

**Today I will take time to rest and
review my week.**

Where have I been thoughtful?

Can I see results from my thoughtfulness?

Am I aware of any thoughtful actions
by other people to me this week?

How do I feel about myself as a result
of my thoughtfulness?

What did I learn this week?

Can I see that I am making a difference in the world?

Another improvement . . . is that we built our gas chambers to accommodate two thousand people at one time.

—Rudolf Hess

It is chilling to remember what human beings have done to other human beings in the past. It is all the more horrifying to know that people are still being tortured and abused today. We must not take any abuse or even the threat of abuse lightly. As soon as we hear of one human being mistreating another, we must take action to expose it and prevent it. We can never be too busy or too complacent to do this.

Today's Thoughtful Action Step/The Suffering of Others

*The source of love is deep in us, and we can help
others realize a lot of happiness. One word,
one action, one thought, can reduce another person's
suffering and bring that person joy.*

—Thicht Naht Hahn

Today I will search out one person
who is suffering and offer that person one
word or action that can help them feel at
peace.

Affirmation/Words and Gestures

One word can change a person's attitude.

One gesture can change a person's day.

Today I will bring my full awareness to my words and gestures, knowing the power they have over myself and others.

Today I will take time to reflect on what the following thought means to me:

Do not avoid contact with suffering or close your eyes before suffering. Do not lose awareness of the existence of suffering in the life of the world. Find ways to be with those who are suffering . . . awaken yourself and others to the reality of suffering in the world.

—A Buddhist Precept for Love in Action

When I take the time to be thoughtful,
I can ask myself this important question:
Who can benefit from my experience?

Today I will give thought to an important book that I read that has been an
inspiration in my life. I will lend this book
to someone who might benefit from it. Or
I can buy another one and give it away.
Or I can simply pass on the title or information.

Today's Thoughtful Action
Step/Release Anger

Today I will find ways to release all
anger and resentments that I am holding
onto from the past so that I can be free to
experience peace in this moment.

I can write a letter or talk to a friend,
family member, clergy, spiritual adviser
or a therapist.

I can make an amend, if it is appropriate, or do a good deed.

I can pray and meditate, or I can ask
for help and trust that help is on the way.

—Ruth Fishel
Five Minutes for World Peace

**Today I will take time to rest and
review my week.**

Have I taken the time to read something that expands my consciousness and
awareness?

Have I put that awareness to work for
others?

Have I taken action when I could to
change something for the better?

I read a poem in the Boston Herald during the late 1930s that made an impression on me. I cut it out and memorized it. I said it every day as I left my home for school and then, later, going to work. On occasions when I am writing or skeptical about my ability to complete a chore I still recite it.

> This day shall I do my work
> With eager heart and cheerful mind
> I may not meet success
> But I shall give all that I have
> Unto my work.
> God, be with me as I labor.

—Anonymous

—Vita Orlano Sinopoli

**Today's Thoughtful Action
Step/Decision to Take Action**

*There are risks and costs to a program of action,
but they are far less than the long-range risks
and costs of comfortable inaction.*

—John F. Kennedy

Where have I been complacent?
Where have I accepted the unacceptable,
wondering when the government, the
boss or someone else will take care of it?

Today I will decide that within one
week I will take an action step involving
an unacceptable condition I see in the
world. I can begin with my own life and
watch how that affects my larger world.

Affirmation/Positive Thinking

*. . . Thoughts always lead to words and
actions. If love is in our heart,
every thought word and deed
can bring about a miracle.
Because understanding is the
very foundation of love, words
and actions that emerge
from our love are always helpful.*

—Thich Nhat Hanh

If left unchallenged, negative thinking becomes a way of life, affecting all we do and say. Today I am making the effort to stop myself every time I have a negative thought. I am making a conscious decision to change it to a positive thought.

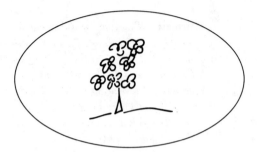

Today I will take time to reflect on
what the following thought means to me:

A tree that reaches past your
embrace grows
from one small seed.
A structure over nine stories high begins
with a handful of earth.
A journey of a thousand miles starts
with a single step.

—Tao 64

When I take the time to be thoughtful, I can consider today's important question: Almost every day we read of at least one young student who has been killed, intentionally or by a random bullet. Each victim leaves behind a grief-stricken family. What act of thoughtfulness can I perform for one of these families? I can send a card or write a letter. What else can I do?

Today's Thoughtful Action Step/Generosity

When I find myself with extra shopping coupons, I will leave them on shelves for others who need those items.

**Today I will take time to rest
and review my week.**

Everyone can do *something* for others. Added together, all these *somethings* become enormous evidence of willingness to take part in moving the world toward peace.

Was I helping this week?
What did I contribute?

When I was going through a very difficult time, someone called me up and played piano music for me on my answering machine. It made me feel very loved, and I never discovered who did it.

—The Editors of Conari Press
Random Acts of Kindness

Today's Thoughtful Action Step/Change

Insanity is doing the same thing over and over again and expecting different results.

Today I will bring my thoughtful awareness to the places in my life where I am stuck.

I will discover one area that can be changed to result in a more peaceful, contented life.

When I make this thoughtful change in my own life, I will be able to share what I have learned from this experience with others.

Affirmation/Doing Nothing

So often we feel as if we need to do something to be helpful. And many times we feel guilty if we do nothing.

There *is* a time and a place for everything.

There *is* time to wait until we are clear in our purpose.

There *is* time to wait before we act, until we are certain that no harm will come from our actions.

Today I will think before I act. Today I will take time to be thoughtful before I take action that can be harmful to others.

Today I will take time to reflect on
what the following thought means to me:

Don't just do something! Sit there!

—Anonymous
Courage to Change

When I take the time to be thoughtful, I can consider today's important question: In the course of our daily lives, there are bound to be upsets and disappointments. Life does not always give us the answers we want to hear. It might even rain on our parade. In spite of all our fist pounding, foot stamping or pouting, we may not get our way.

How can we find harmony in this type of climate?

Is the spiritual path traveled only in sunshine?

Today's Thoughtful Action
Step/Speaking Out

If I know of any human being in danger of being mistreated or abused, I will take the time to do at least one action to prevent it from continuing. This action step can consist of my speaking out directly, writing a letter or making a phone call. I will find a safe but effective protest.

**Today I will take time to rest and
review my week.**

When people around me were out of
sorts, did I do something to help them?
Did I bring thoughtfulness and healing to others this week?
Did I look for my spiritual path?

One moment of just being here . . . being one with someone . . . being fully present together in the moment . . . can make the difference between a good day and a bad day . . . for both of us.

Today's Thoughtful Action
Step/Supporting Companies
that Support the Planet

Today I will go out of my way to research companies that contribute to the health of the planet and the people in it. There are companies who contribute a percentage of their sales or profits to non-profit organizations who do this good work.

When I find this information, I will make sure I buy from these companies and suggest others do the same.

Affirmation/Kind to Myself

Just for today, I will be kind to myself. I will try to live through this day only, and not tackle all my problems at once. I can do something for twelve hours that would appall me if I felt that I had to keep it up for a lifetime.

I will feel better about myself and I will put less pressure on those around me.

—Adapted from Al-Anon Family Group Headquarters, Inc.,© New York, 1972.

Today I will take time to reflect on what the following thought means to me:

God was here all along and the reason that I didn't know it was because I was too busy paying attention to myself.

—Rabbi Lawrence Kushner

When I take the time to be thoughtful,
I can consider today's important question:
Can I be a good listener when I have
something on my own mind?

Can I let go of myself long enough to
listen to a friend and really be there?

Can I really hear a concern of another
when I have concerns of my own?

—Judy Fishel

Today's Thoughtful Action
Step/Letting Someone Help Me

Knowing and accepting our own needs is an act of kindness to ourselves. Allowing ourselves to let someone else help us is a gift to both of us!

Today I will find an area of my life that could use some help. I will put this need out there to the universe and accept help when it comes back to me.

**Today I will take time to rest and
review my week.**

Did I remember that great things
happen because of a lot of little things?

Have I taken time to value my contribution to those little things?

Have I remembered that I am some-
body?

My father always looked forward to wearing a new suit to the office. He left for work feeling two inches taller whenever he had one on. But a different man arrived home that night. He looked tired and three inches shorter.

"Nobody said anything about my new suit today," he'd say. My mother tried to tell him it's hard to say things like "you look nice" or "great suit" to the boss. I always remembered his sad, vulnerable face.

Now I remember that no one is so self-contained or powerful that he or she is above needing a kind word or compliment.

— Mary Littleford

Today's Thoughtful Action
Step/Thank You

Today I will remember a person who has been a positive influence in my life. I will let this person know how much I appreciate him or her by making a phone call or writing a letter. If I cannot reach this person for whatever reason, perhaps I can let a family member or friend know how much that person has helped me.

Affirmation/Honoring
My Commitments

Today I will reflect on any commitments I have made and see if I've carried them out.

If I haven't, I can make a plan to do it.

If I have, I can give myself a pat on the back and continue to make sure that I can fulfill any others that I make in the future.

Today I will take time to reflect on what the following thought means to me:

Good will is the mightiest practical force in the Universe.

—C.F. Dole
Cleveland Address

When I take the time to be thoughtful, I can ask myself this important question: It's one thing to think thoughtful actions. It's another to actually act on them. Have I had a helpful thought and not acted on it?

Today I will remember at least one thoughtful act that I have not put into action yet. I will take the first step to do something about it today.

**Today's Thoughtful Action
Step/Surprise Gift**

Today I will leave a flower in a place where someone will be surprised to find it. I can leave it on the seat of someone's car or on a desk or a pillow. And I can let myself feel good imagining the response!

**Today I will take time to rest and
review my week.**

Have I thought about how important
it is to follow through on my promises?

Have I delighted someone with a small
surprise this week?

Have I honored my conception of God
and the people I think of as gifts of God?

I'm not good at saying no, and recently my accumulated yes's snowballed into an overfilled schedule of responsibilities. One day an elderly church member sobbed and told me his house had been condemned. He was just recovering from surgery and he needed a place to stay for three months.

I remembered the Bible verse ". . . I was a stranger and you invited me in" (Matthew 25:35).

"Oh God, am I supposed to take him home? Where do I stop?" I thought. Then a dear friend gave me a card that is still on my refrigerator: Do not feel total personal responsibility for everything. That's my job. [Signed God.]

—Shirley Pieters Vogel

Today's Thoughtful Action
Step/Thank You

Today I will think about a person in my life whom I have taken for granted. I will go out of my way to acknowledge this person with a verbal thanks, a gift or a card.

Affirmation/Generosity

When we feel angry or resentful about giving to someone, often it is because we think we should give, not because we want to give.

The difference lies in accepting responsibility for the decision. It feels different when we say to ourselves that we *choose* to give something, than when we say we *should* give something. The change in intention makes the difference in how we feel.

Today I choose to give with love.

Today I will take time to reflect on what the following thought means to me:

Every thought we think is creating our future.

—Louise Hay

When I take the time to be thoughtful, I can ask myself this important question: Who can benefit from my experience?

Today I will reflect on a time in my life when I reached a turning point and had to make a significant change. What lessons did I learn? What steps did I take? How did I get through this time? Today I will find a way to share this experience where it can do some good.

Today's Thoughtful Action
Step/Appreciation

There are people who work for our community who are rarely appreciated. People who work for the Sanitation Department or the town dump are probably high on that list! Today I will send a card or letter to the workers in one of these departments, thanking them for making my world a cleaner and more pleasant place to live.

**Today I will take time to rest and
review my week.**

Have I remembered that I cannot do
everything?

Did I remember to do something?

Did I understand that I could do
something small that can make a significant change in someone else's day?

When I see people who are suffering from pain or fear, I pray their lives will be eased and their pain transmuted into hope and a sense of purpose. When I see people who are suffering I am always moved to help. Sometimes, the best help is to do nothing more than hold a hand or give a hug. Hope and purpose must be born from who a person is, deep down, responding to some inner catalyst.

—Sandy Bierig

Today's Thoughtful Action
Step/Forgiveness

Today I will increase my thoughtfulness around the area of forgiveness. I will be more aware of the healing power of forgiveness. If I should make a mistake or hurt someone's feelings, I will simply say "I'm sorry." If I feel I need to add something to that, I will. I'll pray that I can let go of my own ego and my need to be right or perfect. I'll be more thoughtful about how my actions affect others.

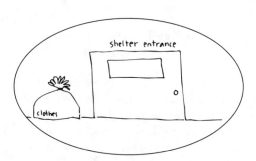

Affirmation/Giving Secretly

Today I will find at least one thing to do for someone else and not tell them! And I will be aware of the feelings I experience as I imagine their reaction!

Today I will take time to reflect on
what the following thought means to me:

*If you have been lifted up by so much
as one grain, then as you go forth,
you are carrying that
grain of spiritual Light out
into the world.*

—Joel S. Goldsmith

When we take the time to be thoughtful, we gain courage to look within. We begin to discover who we really are.

We can look gently and without judgement, learning to accept ourselves totally, just as we are.

As each of us does this, we are more and more able to accept those who are different from us. We are more and more able to accept differences of opinion, people whom we don't understand and even those with whom we disagree.

This is the beginning of inner and outer peace.

**Today's Thoughtful Action
Step/Sharing Myself**

Today I will think about an experience, a book or a quote that has been an inspiration to me. I will then find a way to share it. Is there someone I know who is stuck or having a tough time? Someone who is discouraged or depressed? Today I will look for an opportunity to share myself in a way that will give me more than I am giving away!

**Today I will take time to rest
and review my week.**

Have I touched another person this week?

Have I lost myself in the process?

Did I lessen someone's suffering?

Did I need to receive instead?

Have I learned more about forgiveness?

Owen has AIDS. It first appeared in 1986. At that time people with AIDS survived about two years. But Owen is a caregiver and his father was dying. He had to help the family. After his father died, his brother became ill with AIDS and then died. His grieving mother was distraught. His friend Tom was also dying of AIDS. There was no time for Owen to be ill. His grandmother died, his friend died and finally his mother died. Owen was always there, taking care of the sick. Owen's concern for other people, his caring, kindness and thoughtfulness has turned him into a long-term survivor.

—Marie Stilkind

Today's Thoughtful Action
Step/Taking a Stand

Today I will look for at least one area where I take a stand that can make a difference in the world. I will either make a call, fax or write about my opinion to a person who can do something about it.

Affirmation/Attitude

*Today I can say, "Good morning,
God," instead of
"Good God, it's morning."*

> —Anonymous
> *Courage to Change*

When I change my attitude, I change my whole life. It is as simple as making a decision to stop what I am doing and change direction.

Today I will take time to reflect on
what the following thought means to me:

*The degree of harmony that comes into
your experience is proportionate to
the degree of your
own spiritual development.*

—Joel S. Goldsmith

When I take the time to be thoughtful, I realize that my actions are like a pebble dropped into a small stream. The reverberations are felt in the deepest ocean.

Whatsoever you do unto the least of these,
you do to me.

—Jesus Christ

181

Today's Thoughtful Action Step/Love

Today I will increase my thoughtfulness around the area of love. I will be more aware of love's energy. I will say "I love you" as often as possible, whenever it feels appropriate. I will observe how I feel when I do this and how I perceive my words are being received.

**Today I will take time to rest and
review my week.**

Have I acted as if I matter this week?

Have I practiced changing my own
attitude before expecting it of others?

Have I offered love to the people I
care about?

Am I feeling myself expanding
emotionally?

Besides the noble art of getting things done,
there is the noble art of leaving things undone.
The wisdom of life consists
in the elimination of non-essentials.

—Lin Yutang

What are the things that I continue to do in my life that bring no positive gain?

What are the things I do over and over again that bring discomfort to myself or another?

What are the things that waste my time, money or spirit?

I will focus on these questions as I go through my day and commit to give up at least one of them.

Today's Thoughtful Action
Step/Unexpected Gifts

Around holiday time awareness is high for the people in nursing homes, halfway houses and hospitals. Many people give turkeys at Thanksgiving and presents at Hanukkah and Christmas.

Today I will select an ordinary day to surprise some of those people with gifts for no special occasion other than my thoughts of them!

Affirmation/Simplify Life

*How would you be seeing or doing this
differently if you were willing to
let it be easy?*

—Alan Cohen
Joy Is My Compass

If I let myself, I can make a mountain
out of any molehill! When I think about
being thoughtful, I immediately want to
save the world! Today I will keep it simple, trusting my inner guidance. If I
struggle to figure out which step to take
next, I am depriving myself of any possi-
bility of joy or satisfaction that is part of
spontaneous giving.

Today I will get out of my own way
and act from my heart.

Today I will take time to reflect on
what the following thought means to me:

*'Twas a thief who said the last kind word
to Christ: Christ took the kindness
and forgave the thief.*

—Giuseppe Caponsacchi
The Ring and the Book, VI

When I take the time to be thoughtful, I can ask myself this important question: Who can benefit from my experience?

Where do I find my strength? Where do I turn for answers? Today I will reflect on these questions and ask for guidance so that I can share myself with others who are without strength and answers.

**Today's Thoughtful Action
Step/Affirming Someone**

Today I will find just the right person
who needs a loving message and I will let
them know I am glad they were born!

—Lorraine Franciose

**Today I will take time to rest and
review my week.**

Have I been able to get things done
this week?

Have I kept things in perspective, not
needing to put myself in control of everything?

Do I say "I love you" to my family and
friends often enough?

Have I acknowledged the source of
my strength?

Learning to express the way you feel, physically and emotionally, may be the single most important part of growing up. To release what's going on inside of you helps you to understand and be more thoughtful of others.

—Michael Boisseau

Today's Thoughtful Action
Step/Service

Today I will increase my thoughtfulness around the area of service. I will be more aware of the energy given and received when I am coming from a place of service. I will be helpful to others as often as possible, whenever it feels appropriate. I will observe how I feel when I do this and how I perceive my actions are being received.

Affirmation/Light

There are two ways of spreading light;
to be the candle or the mirror that reflects it.

—Edith Wharton

Today I will do my best to bring light
to the darkness of ignorance, greed and
negativity. Every day of my life I can find
opportunities to do that in small ways.
Big changes come from lots of small ones.

Today I will take time to reflect on
what the following thought means to me:

To live with great wisdom and compassion
is possible for anyone who
genuinely undertakes a
training of their heart and mind.

—Jack Kornfield

When I take the time to be thoughtful,
I can ask myself this important question:
We hear of the tremendous suffering
going on in the world so often that we
become immune to the horror of it! It's all
over the front pages of the newspapers. It
makes up a large portion of our evening
news. It's discussed in every local gather-
ing place.

How often do I think that I will send a
donation or write a letter of protest, but
by the time I get home or wake up, my
good intentions are gone?

What can I do today to help me
remember to follow through with at least
one good intention aimed at someone
else?

Today's Thoughtful Action
Step/Thank You!

Today I will bring my thoughts to someone that I am grateful to have in my life. This person may not have done anything special for me. I just feel better knowing this person.

Today I will take the time to write a note to say thanks. Just a few words to let this person know he or she is special to me.

**Today I will take time to rest and
review my week.**

Have I learned more about gratitude
this week?

Have I tried to bring light to the darkness?

Have I been of service to someone
needing my help?

When we behave in a manner that lacks thoughtfulness and consideration, we are the ones who suffer the most in the long run.

People can move out of our way or out of our lives, but we have to live with ourselves. We take ourselves with us wherever we go. And we might find ourselves to be in a very lonely place.

**Today's Thoughtful Action
Step/Taking Time To Praise**

The next time I see someone do something thoughtful, I'll take the time to acknowledge it!

Affirmation/No More Complaining!

If I feel that I have something to complain about today, I will do so with great thoughtfulness. I can ask myself:

Am I discrediting anyone with this complaint?

Can I state my case without harming anyone or making someone else wrong?

Is there a peaceful way to get satisfaction?

Can this be a situation where no one loses?

I will only speak and act after taking the necessary time to bring thought to all these aspects.

Today I will take time to reflect on
what the following thought means to me:

> *We took them to the edge and*
> *bade them fly. They held on.*
> *Fly we said. They held on.*
> *We pushed them over the edge.*
> *They flew.*

—Guillaume Apollinaire

When I take the time to be thoughtful, I can ask myself this important question: Who can benefit from my experience?

Today I will give thought to a quote that has been an inspiration in my life. I will write it down and pass it on to be an inspiration for someone else.

Today's Thoughtful Action Step/Letting Go

Today I will be careful not to enable someone by doing for them what they can do for themselves.

**Today I will take time to rest and
review my week.**

Have I decided on action steps this
week?

Have I supported the unfolding of the
personality of someone else this week?

Have I seen how much joy I get from
letting go and watching others fly?

Today my thinking is spiritually centered instead of self-centered. I pray for a peaceful world and send peace, love, health and prosperity to those people or situations that I allow to disturb my serenity. My thoughts of love are sent to those who are suffering in any way or manner.

— Nancy Young Williams

Today's Thoughtful Action
Step/Reaching Out

Thoughtfulness brings an awareness of self and others. Today I will reach out to at least one other person in a thoughtful way, either through a thank you, an encouraging word, a note or a compliment truly given.

—Ann Harmon

Affirmation/Think Before You Act

Today I will think before I act.
Today I will take time to be thoughtful
before I take action that can be harmful to
others.

Today I will take time to reflect on
what the following thought means to me:

*In reality, heroes are heroic
because they, despite their weaknesses —
and sometimes because of
them — do great things.*

—Benjamin Hoff

When I take the time to be thoughtful, I can ask myself this important question: What can I let go of in my life that does not serve the good of all human beings?

What products can I stop buying?

What companies, stores and restaurants can I stop supporting?

I can continue to stay aware and mindful so that I support only people who cooperate in a way that supports the dignity of all people.

In my humble opinion, noncooperation
with evil is as much a duty
as is cooperation with good.

—Gandhi

Today's Thoughtful Action
Step/Connect with Someone

And then he gave a long sigh and said,
"I wish Pooh were here.
It's so much more friendly
with two."

—A.A. Milne
Winnie the Pooh

Today I will think of one person who is lonely. If there is not someone immediately in my life at this time who is lonely, I won't have to look far. I can go to a shelter, a nursing home or a hospital.

Today I will make a connection with someone.

**Today I will take time to rest and
review my week.**

Have I reached out this week to someone in need of contact with another
human being?

Have I tried, when I could, even in a
small way, to lessen suffering some-
where?

If I have not been able to help, have I
remembered not to harm?

Today I am willing to see someone else's anger as an expression of their pain and respond to it as a call for help. When I begin to respond with compassion and understanding to negative behavior, I experience more peace and harmony in my own life.

Today I release my need to "fix" anyone; I will remember that when anyone feels pushed, their impulse is to resist. As I let go of my need for them to change and accept them as they are, miracles occur naturally.

—Joy Adams

Today's Thoughtful Action Step/Simplify

Today I will look through my closet, choosing to give away at least one piece of clothing I have not worn for over a year. I will be acting thoughtfully to myself and to someone who can benefit from receiving my clothes.

Affirmation/Faith

Today I know that God is guiding me toward peace and calm. I know that anything that upsets this feeling is not permanent and will pass.

Today I will not let my upsets keep me from seeing the good in others. I will not let my upsets construct walls between myself and other people.

Today I will take time to reflect on
what the following thought means to me:

*I do not agree with a word that you say,
but I will defend to the death
your right to say it.*

—Voltaire

When I take the time to be thoughtful,
I can ask myself this important question:
Is there a person I can ride with today,
rather than take my own car alone?

Am I willing to give up convenience
for the sake of cutting down pollution
and crowded roads?

**Today's Thoughtful Action
Step/Loving Eyes**

We all know about the pain and suffering of humanity, but how often do we take the time to be grateful for the good in our lives? How often do we bless the people who support, love and encourage us, through easy and difficult times?

When I allow myself kindness, good friends and lots of love and gentleness, I can be the person I am called to be.

Today I will look upon the world with loving eyes and not close my eyes to pain and suffering, recognizing that the world is also filled with goodness!

—Linda Hansen

**Today I will take time to rest and
review my week.**

Am I creating new ways to be in the
world or am I still using the same old
ones?

Am I reaching out or turning inward?

Am I conscious of the ways in which I
affect others, or do I go on, ignorant of
the needs of those around me?

When I do not see immediate results
from my new thoughtful actions and affirmations, I will remember this saying:

Good travels at a snail's pace.
Those who want to do good are not selfish.
They are not in a hurry,
they know that to impregnate
people to do good requires a long time.

—Gandhi

Today's Thoughtful Action
Step/Kind to Myself

_Just for today, I will be kind to myself.
I will have a quiet half hour by myself
and relax. During this half hour,
I will try to get a better
perspective on my life._

—Anonymous,
Courage to Change

Affirmation/Think Before You Speak

I will be careful of my speech and actions today. I will slow down enough whenever possible so that I can think before I speak and act. In this way I have a better chance of not hurting anyone or creating any serious harm in my life or anyone else's.

Today I will take time to reflect on
what the following thought means to me:

God, who neither causes or prevents tragedies,
helps by inspiring people to help.
As a nineteenth-century Hasidic
rabbi once put it,
"human beings are God's language."

—Rabbi Harold Kushner

When I take the time to be thoughtful, I can consider today's important questions:

Where have I been careless?

Where have I spoken without thought?

Have I been sarcastic?

Have I shown disrespect to anyone?

Can I correct anything I have done by making amends?

**Today's Thoughtful Action
Step/Affirm Someone!**

So many people are quietly doing wonderful things. Today I will go out of my way to make sure I acknowledge a thoughtful or courageous act. We need to tell each other more often how great we really are!

Today I will take time to rest and review my week.

Have I taken time to be careful about how I speak to others?

Do I tell other people enough that they are terrific?

Have I listened to God's message as it comes to me through others?

When my partner began her job as co-director of a chemical dependency program for women many years ago, she was given simple but profound advice.

She was told to imagine her clients as if they were dough needing to be shaped into loaves of bread. She possessed the magic, the yeast, that would help them rise. The ingredient was praise. All she had to do was praise, praise, praise, and the women would grow, grow, grow into their full potential.

It is amazing how effective praise can be to the person who needs support to take the next step not to give up!

Today's Thoughtful Action Step/Helping Someone Feel Comfortable

When I am in a room full of people, I will look for a person who has no one to talk to, and I will say hello and share a smile.

Affirmation/Music

Music often removes the barriers between people. A love song, a great symphony, an operatic aria—these things touch almost everyone, bringing us just a little closer to each other as human beings.

Today I will bring my awareness to areas where music could make a difference and add quality to the moment. Today I will consider ways that music can make a positive change in my life.

Today I will take time to reflect on
what the following thought means to me:

Make your space as beautiful as you can,
Because the Great Spirit chooses
where it will dwell,
And it will always choose
beauty over chaos.

—Native American saying

When I take the time to be thoughtful,
I can consider today's important questions:

What is spirituality to me?

Am I careful not to inflict my ideas on others, but do I share them, without embarrassment, when appropriate?

Am I able to listen openly to others' point of view and not insist that they share mine?

We ought not to insist on everybody following
in our footsteps, nor to take upon ourselves
to give instructions in spirituality
when, perhaps, we do not even
know what it is.

—Teresa of Avila

Today's Thoughtful Action
Step/Handmade Gifts

Today I will begin making a gift rather than buying one for someone. It doesn't have to be complicated or look professional. Just the fact that I am taking the time to do it myself will have more meaning to the person I am giving it to than any manufactured present.

**Today I will take time to rest and
review my week.**

Was I gentle enough with myself this
week?

Did I speak up in support of my
beliefs?

Was I wasteful of my resources?

Did I reach out to help anyone?

There are some situations where I would like to do something to be thoughtful and I find, to my frustration, that I can't. I cannot always have the energy I want or the answers or the time.

These days can be difficult.

These are the times to pause and rest.

These are the times when the most thoughtful thing I can do is have patience and acceptance.

The best thing to do is to be gentle with myself, remembering that these times will not last and I am a human being, not a robot.

—Ruth Fishel
Time for Joy

233

Today's Thoughtful Action
Step/Thoughtfulness for the Planet

Today I will do something positive to express my protest against the destruction of the rain forest. I can write a letter, make a phone call or begin a local petition. I can tell others to do the same.

The more people who take action at the same time, the more we can change the energy of the universe and make a difference.

Affirmation/Slowing Down

*It empowers us to transcend the powerful
influences of urgency, expediency,
and instant gratification
in the moment of choice.*

—Stephen R. Covey

Rushing to act can leave us in stress
and chaos. Thoughtless action can be
harmful to others and ourselves. Choices
made to satify our egos and senses, while
feeling good in the moment, can lead to
future suffering.

Today I am taking time to consider
what is right for the highest good for all
concerned. Today I am taking time to be
thoughtful and then acting from a place of
peace and inner knowing.

Today I will take time to reflect on what the following thought means to me:

*Aware of the suffering caused by
the destruction of life,
I vow to cultivate compassion and learn
ways to protect the lives of people,
animals, plants and minerals.*

—First Buddhist precept

When I take the time to be thoughtful, I can consider today's important question: Are there situations in my life draining me? Are there situations or people that I should let go so I will have more energy for situations and people that are more important?

Today's Thoughtful Action
Step/Shopping for Someone Sick

I will look around today for an opportunity to help someone who can't do their own shopping. If I do know of anyone, I I can ask around to see if someone else knows a person who has this need. Once I have brought thought to my intention, the wheels are in motion and the right person will appear when the time is right.

....

....

....

....

....

**Today I will take time to rest and
review my week.**

Have I taken the time to help others
grow by praising them?

Did I work on improving the condition of my own heart and mind this week?

Did I add quality to even brief
moments through music?

To every thing there is a season,
and a time to every purpose under the heaven.
A time to be born, and
a time to die;
A time to weep, and
a time to laugh;
a time to mourn, and
a time to dance;
A time to keep silence and
a time to speak.

—Ecclesiastes

**Today's Thoughtful Action
Step/Service with a Smile**

There are times when I want to be thoughtful even if I am not in a good mood. If I find myself inclined to moan or complain today, I will smile instead. I do not have to make someone else feel bad for me or guilty for my mood.

Affirmation/Being a Friend

It is always darkest just before the day dawneth.

—Thomas Fuller

There are days when it is difficult for anyone to stay positive. There are days when people feel like giving up. You might know someone who thinks that destructive actions or addictions might appear to be their only answer.

When this happens, sometimes there is nothing we can do but be a friend.

We can suggest treatment or therapy, but we cannot be their therapist.

Today I can turn a friend over to someone else when I cannot be of no help.

Today I will take time to reflect on
what the following thought means to me:

*When you understand, you cannot help
but love. You cannot get angry. To develop
understanding, you have to practice
looking at all living beings
with the eyes of compassion.
When you understand, you love.
And when you love, you naturally
act in a way that can relieve
the suffering of people.*

—Thich Nhat Hanh

When I take the time to be thoughtful,
I can discover where each moment fits
into the highest good for all concerned.

**Today's Thoughtful Action
Step/Helping Parents**

People with small children sometimes
need an extra boost during the particularly weary winter months or a stormy spell.
I can perk things up with a plant. I can
watch the kids for a while so that Mom or
Dad can shop, go to a movie or rest.

**Today I will take time to rest and
review my week.**

Have my actions spoken of love this
week?

Have I contributed, even in small
ways, to the good of my community?

Have I practiced compassion for all
living things?

Some time ago, I was feeling very lonely and unlovable. Someone noticed this and sent me a cheerful card. The unexpected gift brightened my spirits beyond belief. Today I get great joy when I shop for greeting cards, each a beautiful work of art. The real joy comes from sending one of these cards to someone in need. When I do it, I know I am passing on the wonderful gift that was given to me, knowing that someone cares about how I feel.

—Diane Austin

Today's Thoughtful Action
Step/Showing Thoughtfulness
to People I Don't Like

How much easier it is to give something to a person we like! Not that giving is always easy. There are times when it is difficult to give, even if we are giving to someone we care about. We might be having a hard time financially, or feeling as if we don't have enough of something ourselves. We might be in a fearful place and lack faith and trust.

Today I will practice giving to someone I don't care about. Today I will give something away, whether it be something material or my time or patience.

Affirmation/Health

I affirm you, Divine Health,
flowing through me, permeating
all my body parts and driving
away any impurities or negativity
so that each part of my body
performs in perfect harmony
and is in tune with
the infinite.

—F. Winston Williams

I will see to my physical well-being
today and help one other person take care
of theirs. We will both move toward God.

Today I will take time to reflect on
what the following thought means to me:

*Good thoughts are like fresh popcorn
in a pan that is too small
on a hot stove,
on a cold winter's evening . . .
overflowing and delicious!*

—Carol Warth Plummer

When I take the time to be thoughtful,
I can consider today's important question:

Do I truly do my best to live by the
values I know are important?

Do I forgive myself and others when
we are less than perfect?

**Today's Thoughtful Action
Step/Sharing**

I have been given gifts which will make me feel fulfilled only when I have used them for others as well as for myself. Keeping my talents only to myself is a waste of my ability to become truly whole.

Today I will go out of my way to make sure that I share at least one of my gifts with someone else.

—Ruth Fishel
Time for Joy

**Today I will take time to rest and
review my week.**

Did I take the time to consider how
others might be feeling this week?

Did I take care of myself this week?

Have I examined my own behaviors to
see if they have placed burdens on the
lives of others?

When I am jealous or angry at someone, I find the Buddhist Mettaloving-kindness prayer to be very effective. It is a kind action I can take for myself and the person for whom I have these negative feelings. I send thoughts of loving kindness to this other person.

May you be happy.
May you be peaceful.
May you be free from suffering.
As I want to be happy, peaceful, and free from suffering,
may you be happy, peaceful,
and free from suffering.

I am then no longer locked into negative energy and I am free to take proper and effective action.

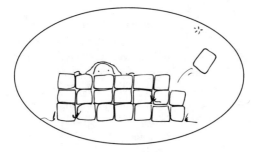

**Today's Thoughtful Action
Step/Remove Barriers**

Today I will continue to remove any barriers that are between myself and my interconnectedness with others. Is there someone to be forgiven? Is there a debt to pay? Is there a thank you to write? If there is any action step I can take, I will do it today.

Affirmation/Faith

Today I will be aware not to judge others when they act "less than perfect." As I improve in my ability to accept others just as they are, I am finding more and more peace in my relationships. I can also expect others to accept me as I am.

Today I will take time to reflect on
what the following thought means to me:

Aware of the suffering caused by the exploitation,
social injustice, stealing and oppression,
I vow to cultivate loving kindness and
learn ways to work for the well-being
of people, animals, plants and minerals.

—Second Buddhist precept

When I take the time to be thoughtful,
I can consider today's important question:

Are there areas where I lack tolerance
of another's point of view?

Do I still react to any old tapes of
prejudice?

Where do I feel superior or inferior?

Today I will question my belief system
and observe my reactions.

Tolerance is the positive and cordial effort
to understand another's beliefs, practices,
and habits without necessarily sharing or
accepting them. Tolerance quickens
our appreciation and increases our respect
for a neighbor's point of view.

—Rabbi Joshua Loth Liebman

Today's Thoughtful Action
Step/Kindness to Animals

From now on I will be very careful about cutting the plastic rings holding six-packs together. Birds and small animals get caught in them. Dolphins and turtles swallow and choke on them. Today I will make others aware of this situation to further alleviate the suffering in the universe.

**Today I will take time to rest and
review my week.**

When have I been judgmental of others this week?

Am I still just reacting in my relationships or am I beginning to initiate change?

Our world is showing wounds from years of abuse and neglect. The alarming effects of depleted resources are apparent. Many people have forgotten about living for principles such as loving our neighbors and putting an end to suffering. They have died instead for espousing ideologies such as those of the Third Reich or Communist Russia. It is time to heal our world by healing our brothers and sisters.

Today's Thoughtful Action
Step/Beautify the Community

Some towns have "Daffodil Days" in the fall of each year. People buy bulbs, keeping half for themselves and donating the other half to the town to plant along the sides of the roads.

It makes driving a joy in the spring.

It's a wonderful idea! Wouldn't it be great if towns all over the country started using this idea?

Today I will pass this idea on to someone who can do something about it!

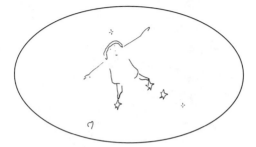

Affirmation/Balancing

To be ourselves causes us to be exiled by
many others, and yet to comply
with what others want
causes us to be exiled from ourselves.

—Clarissa Pinkola Estes, Ph.D.

Today I will try to find the balance
point between the two worlds, trying not
to lose sight of either.

Today I will take time to reflect on
what the following thought means to me:

> *The decisive question in a*
> *human being's life is this:*
> *Am I related to something*
> *infinite or not?*

—Carl Jung

When I take the time to be thoughtful, I can consider today's important question: I am not always the one most able to accomplish things that need to be done. This is not easy to admit.

Is there something I am doing that could be better handled by someone else?

Is there someone I can ask to step in for me?

Is there someone I can ask for help?

Today's Thoughtful Action
Step/Meditation

I start my day in quiet meditation. Meditation is an action step. Meditation is being fully aware and alive in each moment.

I feel myself becoming still and at peace.

I feel connected to everyone reading this book today.

I feel the power of all positive and loving people in the world becoming more and more thoughtful.

I feel myself changing as we are changing the world.

**Today I will take time to rest and
review my week.**

Have I let others know I love them
this week?

Have I reflected on the principles I follow?

Have I been compassionate of others?

Have I valued the abilities of others?

For people with AIDS, pets provide warmth, love and understanding when people may fail to do so. One man I know was able to keep his dog with him almost to the end of his days. Others with AIDS may not be so lucky and they are deprived of the unconditional love their "best friend" can give them. It can be difficult and expensive to look after a pet when illness is draining the resources.

Pets Are Wonderful Support (PAWS) is a rapidly growing organization that helps people with AIDS care for their pets. It is a thoughtful act from one animal lover to another.

— Marie Stilkind

Today's Thoughtful Action
Step/Communication

Today I will discover one person who
can benefit from my call or visit. I will not
put this off for another day.

Affirmation/Listen

I will be more aware of myself as a listener today. Do I really hear the person who is talking to me?

Am I instead thinking of what I am going to say when they are finished? Or am I daydreaming or planning?

I will pay attention to both sides of the conversation today, not just the one side that has to do with me!

Today I will take time to reflect on what the following thought means to me:

> *Who sees his Lord*
> *Within every creature,*
> *Deathlessly dwelling*
> *Amidst the mortal:*
> *That man sees truly.*

—Krishna

When I take the time to be thoughtful, I can consider today's important question: How can I get the most out of today?

What do I need to avoid?

What do I consider really important in my relationships with those I love?

What do I tell myself about those I love?

—Dr. Nelson Boswell
Inner Peace, Inner Power

**Today's Thoughtful Action
Step/Handmade Gifts**

Today I will make a greeting card rather than buying one. I can do this by hand or even on my computer if I have a program for this. It doesn't have to be a work of art, just an act of love and thoughtfulness. It will mean much more than any mass-produced greeting card could ever mean!

**Today I will take time to rest
and review my week.**

Have I looked for what I have in common with others rather than obvious differences?

Have I sought God in my enemies as well as my friends?

Today name your guardian angels. I did! "Thoughtfulness" and "Kindness." Tomorrow I'll name the rest!!!

—Carol Warth Plummer

**Today's Thoughtful Action
Step/Touch With Love**

Today I will touch someone with love
through my words, actions or thoughts.

Affirmation/Be Positive!

Today I will fight any tendency I have to be negative by bringing a positive attitude to whatever I do. That way, I will be positive with the people in my life.

Today I will take time to reflect on what the following thought means to me:

*I do not believe that an individual
may gain spiritually while those who
surround him suffer . . .
I believe in the essential unity of man and
for that matter, of all that lives.
Therefore, I believe
that if one man gains spiritually,
the whole world gains with him
and if one man falls,
the whole world falls to that extent.*

—Gandhi

When I take the time to be thoughtful, I can consider today's important questions:

Do I contribute anything to the destruction of our planet?

Do I ever throw trash out the car window?

Do I recycle my plastic bags?

If I see a bottle in the road do I pick it up or do I wait for someone else to do it?

Today's Thoughtful Action
Step/Connection

The simple words "Just thinking about you" can go a long way to brighten up someone's day.

Today I will give some thought to a person who has been going through a particularly difficult time. If this is someone I will see today, I will take the time to put my hand on their shoulder and let them know I have been thinking about them.

If I do not see them, I will touch them with these words anyway, communicating by mail, phone or fax.

**Today I will take time to rest
and review my week.**

Have I been able to be more positive
than negative this week?

Did I contribute in some way to the
well-being of the planet?

Have I been as thoughtful of myself as
I have been of others this week?

I was deeply touched by the thought-fulness of some friends when they called or sent cards on the anniversary and first birthday after my son's death. I was amazed that they were aware of my pain, which was especially deep around these occasions. It was so very thoughtful of them to take time out from their busy day to let me know they were thinking of me.

People's lives are usually full of support from friends and family in the early days after a death. It is so easy to forget the ongoing pain once the funeral is over. Our own lives are full of everyday living, while the mourner's life is still full of grief.

Today I turn my thoughts to someone who would benefit from a caring word, a call or a card.

Today's Thoughtful Action
Step/Thoughtfulness for the Planet

Today I will do something positive to express my protest against fighting going on in the world. I can write a letter, make a phone call or begin a local petition. I can tell others to do the same.

When more and more people take action at the same time, they can change the energy of the universe and make a difference. Today I will make sure to stay on the side of positive action.

Affirmation/This Day for Me

On days that you feel you have nothing to give, stop. Do something thoughtful for yourself! Give this day to yourself. Be kind to yourself. Do at least one thing you like to do. You can take a warm bath or curl up with a book.

Whatever helps you to feel good, do it! Even if it's only for ten minutes. And if there is nothing you can think to do, just be with what is going on, without struggle or judgment. Give yourself permission to be just the way you are at any given moment.

And rest in the knowledge that nothing is forever and this too will change.

I'm giving this day to myself!

Today I will take time to reflect on
what the following thought means to me:

*A healed mind does not plan.
It carries out the plans it receives by
listening to Wisdom that is
not its own. It waits until it has been taught
what should be done and then proceeds to do it.
It does not depend on itself for anything except its
adequacy to fulfill the plans assigned to it."*

—*A Course in Miracles*

When I take the time to be thoughtful,
I can consider today's important question:
  Can I find someone today who is
down, disillusioned and hopeless? Can I
find someone I can inspire?

Scientists tell us that our body is
constantly rebuilding and curing itself.
When the body is fed the mental picture
of wholeness, it builds its cells
according to that picture, whereas when fed
thoughts of hopelessness and incurability,
the body builds the cells according to
that mental picture.

—Katherine Ponder

**Today's Thoughtful Action
Step/Thoughtfulness for the Planet**

Whenever possible I will carry a ceramic or china cup with me for my coffee. In this way I do not have to use Styrofoam cups that do not break down and leave plastic pellets in our earth forever!

**Today I will take time to rest and
review my week.**

Have I acted in a healing way on my
awareness of another's pain?

Have I taken time to stop and rest and
take care of myself when I needed it?

Have I put my good ideas into action
when possible?

If we are facing in the right direction,
all we have to do is keep on walking.

—An ancient Buddhist expression

There are days when I do not feel directed to be thoughtful. There are some days when I am bogged down with the chaos and confusion I have created or have allowed others to create in my life.

My own needs and wants shine before me. My own fears keep me in pain and darkness.

On these days I need to remember that I am on a spiritual path and I need to continue to have faith. As long as I continue to ask for guidance from a Power greater than myself, I will be shown the way.

—Ruth Fishel
Time for Joy

Today's Thoughtful Action Step/Fun!

The path of thoughtfulness and giving does not have to exclude fun! I can still be on a spiritual path and do wonderful, light things in my life! The path does not have to be a burden.

Today I will remember to have balance in my life!

Today I will give thought as to how I can bring fun into someone else's life and share it with them!

Affirmation/Positive Actions

Thoughts without actions are burdens,
but once the action takes place,
they are lifted beyond the burden...

—Louis Gittner

Good intentions not carried out lead to guilt. Guilt leads to low self-esteem. Guilt and low self-esteem pull us down, making us feel unworthy and depressed, separated from our fellow human beings.

Today I will act on one positive, unselfish thought, even if it means giving up something I want or need. I will watch myself feel lighter as my self-esteem rises! I will let myself feel the connection I have with others.

Today I will take time to reflect on
what the following thought means to me:

*It is no good hearing an inner voice
or getting an inner prompting
if you do not immediately act
on that inner prompting.*

—David Spangler

When I take the time to be thoughtful,
I can consider today's important idea.

Shall I take the difficult path or the easy path today?

What am I holding onto that I no longer need that could help someone else?

Are there clothes I haven't worn in years?

Is there money that could serve someone else?

Can I reach for a power greater than myself to help me let go?

> *The path of gradual relinquishment*
> *of things hindering spiritual progress*
> *is a difficult path; for only when*
> *relinquishment is complete do the*
> *rewards really come. The path of quick*
> *relinquishment is an easy path,*
> *for it brings immediate results.*

—Peace Pilgrim

Today's Thoughtful Action
Step/Listening

*Listening is a magnetic and strange thing
a creative force. Friends who listen to us
are the ones we move toward,
and we want to sit in their radius.
When we are listened to, it creates us,
and it makes us unfold and expand.*

—Karl Menninger

We all need a place to vent our emotions, a place to talk.

Today I will be a positive and loving force in someone else's life. Today I will be a safe place for someone to release their burden.

Today I will help someone unfold and expand.

**Today I will take time to rest and
review my week.**

Have I had fun this week?

Have I laughed and shared my laughter with others?

Have I followed through with my ideas when they were a little inconvenient?

Have I been a friend?

Lately, whenever I think of thought-fulness, my attention shifts quickly to for-getfulness . . . and I don't like how this feels. It reminds me just how often I for-get to be thoughtful . . . I beat myself up with this! This self-shaming incapacitates me and I am paralyzed by shame and guilt.

This is no way to treat people!

This is no way to treat me!

I now commit to being more thought-ful to myself and for today end this ongo-ing self-punishment and abuse. I commit to "turn over" this defect of mine and risk allowing another, more gentle and yet, more powerful, presence to take the place of my self-abuser.

I resolve to do this, one day at a time.

—Kula

Today's Thoughtful Action
Step/Changing Negative Tapes

*Whatever the problem is, it comes from a thought
pattern and thought patterns can be changed.*

—Louise Hay

If I think I am worthless and have
nothing to give, it is my thinking that is
wrong, not me.

As I become more and more thoughtful and am able to listen to these negative,
self-defeating tapes, I can turn them
around with positive affirmations. The
next time I think I have nothing to give
anyone else, I will say **stop!** And I will ask
for guidance to get out of my own negativity and reach out to someone else.

Affirmation/Present Awareness

When I live in the now, I feel no real pain from the past. Imagined fear of the future can't harm me. I am at peace with God, myself and the world.

Today I will bring my awareness to where I am in each moment, growing in my ability to live a life of peace.

—Joan Burka

Today I will take time to reflect on what the following thought means to me:

Aware of the suffering caused by unmindful speech and the inability to listen to others, I vow to cultivate loving speech and deep listening in order to bring joy and happiness to others and relieve others of their suffering. I will refrain from uttering words that can cause division or discord, or that can cause the family or the community to break.

—Fourth Buddhist precept

When I take the time to be thoughtful,
I can consider today's important questions:

Can I be thoughtful of others when I
am needy or in pain?

Can I give to others when I think I
don't have enough for myself?

Today's Thoughtful Action
Step/Adventure

Today I will invite a friend to share an adventure with me. It doesn't need to cost a lot of money or take a lot of time. A walk in the park, a visit to a museum or sharing a sundae at the ice cream parlor. These are joys not to be taken lightly and are most fun when shared.

> Today I will take time to rest and
> review my week.

Have I taken myself too seriously this
week?

Have I allowed myself to be myself?

Have I joined with a friend to create
memories?

To be the recipient of someone's thoughtfulness can create a sense of well-being and the lasting warmth of long-remembered memories.

I recall a time in my life during which I was in severe emotional pain. One morning I woke up to find my thirteen-year-old daughter sleeping on the floor beside my bed. When I questioned her about this she quietly told me that she wanted to be near me because she knew I was hurting, but she didn't want to risk disturbing my sleep. The memory of this thoughtful expression of her love and concern still brings tears of gratitude eighteen years later.

— Barbara Thomas

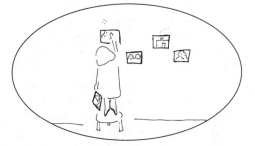

**Today's Thoughtful Action
Step/Photographs**

I can take pictures of special events in my life and, when they are developed, arrange them attractively and present them to my friends and family. Such keepsakes are priceless.

—Diana Smith

Affirmation/Expanding My Mind

*Every now and then a [person's] mind
is stretched by a new idea and
sensation, and [it] never
shrinks back to its former dimensions.*

—Oliver Wendell Holmes

Today I am letting my mind expand by
generating positive, affirming thoughts! I
know that this practice is changing and
developing me as a human being, capable
of doing more positive good every day.

Today I will take time to reflect on
what the following thought means to me:

*Aware of the suffering caused by
sexual misconduct, I vow to cultivate
responsibility and learn
ways to protect the safety and integrity
of individuals, couples, families and
society . . . I will do
everything in my power to protect
children from sexual abuse and to
prevent couples and families from
being broken by
sexual misconduct.*

—Third Buddhist precept

When I take the time to be thoughtful, I can consider today's important idea:

There is someone out there today who needs my help. There is someone who is ready to give up, to quit.

How can I inspire this person?

Do I have a word, a touch or a smile?

Today I will remember the power of love and pass it on when I am led to someone else in need.

Today I will find someone who needs my love.

Today I will share my strength, hope and experience so that someone else can have another chance.

Love builds highways out of dead ends.

—Louis Gittner

Today's Thoughtful Action
Step/Touching Someone
In A Loving Way

For both the individual and the nation,
what should be most dreaded is
not the loss of power but the loss of feeling.
What is happening today is the entire society is
undergoing a decline in sensitivity to
beauty, sensitivity to brutality, sensitivity
to the possibilities of deeper living.

—Norman Cousins

Today I will do something to touch
someone in a loving and heartfelt way. I
can leave them flowers, write a note or
choose another way to reach them so that
they will feel it in their hearts.

**Today I will take time to rest and
review my week.**

Have I thought of some tangible way
to reach out to others this week?

Has my love been clearly stated?

Have I valued my sensitivity to the
feelings of others?

I often marvel at how one thought can make an impact on the world if it is put into action. I am reminded of how Mahatma Gandhi brought the nonviolent movement to the modern world, how Martin Luther King, Jr. brought it to America and how Rosa Parks acted in the civil rights movement.

Though not all of us are so influential, our thoughts can still point the way to good works.

Today I will be attentive to my thoughts, wondering if one of them would benefit my neighbor and should be acted upon.

—Marian Veilleumier

Today's Thoughtful Action
Step/Investments

I will look into the investments of my neighborhood bank. Are they investing the depositor's money in oil companies that harm the ocean or newspaper and paper companies that destroy the rain forests? I can be more thoughtful of all the ramifications of where I spend and save my money. I can change to a bank that is also aware.

Affirmation/Don't Procrastinate!

I feel better and better about myself when I don't procrastinate! Today I am discovering the freedom in completing at least one act of communication, whether it be a card, letter, visit, fax or call.

Today I will take time to reflect on
what the following thought means to me:

The mind grows by what it feeds on.

—J.G. Holland
American Novelist/Poet

When I take the time to be thoughtful, I can consider today's important questions:

I have learned that God speaks to me through other people. Have I taken the time to listen to others this week?

Am I open to what other people say to me?

Today's Thoughtful Action
Step/Asking for Help

*Life only demands from the strength
you possess. Only one feat is possible
—not to have to run away.*

—Dag Hammarskjöld

Sometimes we feel called upon to do more than we think we can do. We must remember that everything we think we "should" be doing does not have to be done now. And it does not mean that we have to do everything alone.

There are days when we cannot always do what we want. Some days do not go our way. We cannot always play or have a good time.

Today I will remember to ask for help when I need it.

Today I will remember to be reasonable in my expectations and goals.

**Today I will take time to rest and
review my week.**

Have I put off doing things I should
have done right away?

Have I been reasonable in my expectations of others?

Have I asked for help or have I let my
pride stand in my way?

Thoughtfulness is giving another enough time and encouragement to come to their own truth.

—Kathleen Moulton

We often think we have the answers for another person. "If only they will listen to us," we think. Or "If they would just take our advice they could be so much happier."

Each of us is responsible for our choices. This is how we create the life we seek. Our lessons come from observing the results of our choices.

We are most thoughtful when we let go of the results of our suggestions. We are most thoughtful when we let others learn from their choices as well.

Today's Thoughtful Action
Step/Message

Today I will leave a loving message on someone's answering machine so that he can begin or end his day knowing someone cares.

Affirmation/Miracles

Today I am spending time making a list of all the miracles I can think of that have occurred in my life. I will carry this list with me or put it in a place that is visible so that I can refer to it when self-pity might appear as an unwelcome guest.

Today I will take time to reflect on
what the following thought means to me:

*Let one therefore keep the mind pure,
for what [people] think, that they become.*

—The Upanishads

When I take the time to be thoughtful,
I can consider today's important question:

Fulfilling our dreams requires that we take action on their behalf. That is what Ghandi did when he first decided not to meet violence with violence. It is what Martin Luther King, Jr. did when he began preaching in his church. It is what the early Americans did when they engaged the British in Concord.

Where can I begin today?

If you build it, they will come.

—*Field of Dreams*

**Today's Thoughtful Action
Step/Reaching Out to the Elderly**

From now on I will be more conscious
of elderly people I pass in the supermar-
ket or mall. Sometimes they look so lonely. It takes nothing away from me to offer
a warm hello and it may give them so
much!

**Today I will take time to rest and
review my week.**

Have I been thoughtful to people of all
ages this week?
Have I respected people as they are?
Have I been open to miracles?

*If you cannot be compassionate to yourself,
you will not be able to be
compassionate to others.*

—Thich Nhat Hanh

Love of others begins with love of self. It is so important that our children are loved as babies so that they develop this quality of self-love. In turn, it is the energy that connects humans to each other and is the foundation of all truly great ideas.

**Today's Thoughtful Action
Step/Visualization**

Today I am picturing myself flooded in
the glow of a powerful bright light that is
guiding me on my path of compassion and
service.

Affirmation/Thinking About Community

Today I will be more thoughtful about other people in my life, remembering that God speaks through them. When I am focused on myself, I cannot hear God. Today is a day to focus on my community and the people in it. Today is the day to open up to others, knowing that when I do this I am connected to the God of my understanding.

Today I will take time to reflect on
what the following thought means to me:

*Aware of the suffering caused by
unmindful consumption, I vow to cultivate good
health, both physical and mental,
for myself, my family and my society by
practicing mindful eating,
drinking and consuming.
I vow to ingest only items that
preserve peace, well-being and joy in
my body, in my consciousness
and in the collective body of my
family and society.*

—Fifth Buddhist precept

When I take the time to be thoughtful, I enter into a deeper connection with my inner spirit. I reach a greater awareness of my connection with everything in the universe.

I feel one with all beings.

I know I am not alone.

Today's Thoughtful Action
Step/Helping the Sick or the Elderly

I will be aware of the sick and the elderly when I have my lawn mower or shovel out. I will be aware of them when I clean up after a storm, flood, hurricane or earthquake. I will add the elderly and people who can't help themselves to my list of what must be done when there is an emergency.

**Today I will take time to rest and
review my week.**

Have I been thoughtful of the elderly
this week and taken action with at least
one of my thoughts?

Have I been shown compassion to
myself in any new way?

What did I learn this week?

Am I making a difference in the
world?

We must learn to accept disagreement. We must learn to respect other points of view, or other perspectives. We can find mutual harmony and peace if we can learn to agree to disagree. As we begin to learn this on a personal level, agreeing to disagree without an argument, we can then pass this lesson along to our friends, neighbors, family and co-workers.

As we begin to accomplish this on a daily, individual basis, we are contributing toward peace for all humanity.

Today's Thoughtful Action Step/Service

    I saw the following sign posted above the gas pump at a local gas station:

    We pump self-serve gas at self-serve prices for vehicles with handicap or disabled veterans plates.

    What a wonderful service! Today I can pass this idea on to others.

Affirmation/Being Present

Today I will be fully present. I will be ready when the moment comes for me to give of myself with thoughtfulness.

Today I will take time to reflect on what the following thought means to me:

Was hilft laufen, wenn man nicht auf den rechten Weg ist?
What is the use of running when we are not on the right way?

—German proverb

When I take the time to be thoughtful, I can consider today's important questions:

What have I been accusing someone else of not doing that I can do myself?

Where can I be responsible today?

Can I take an action step to correct an upset or a wrongdoing?

> *I thought, "Why doesn't someone do*
> *something about this?"*
> *And then I realized I am someone.*

— Unknown

Today's Thoughtful Action
Step/Relieving Another

So many people working in service positions must work on holidays. Today I will find someone I am able to replace and offer the gift of relief for a future holiday. If I do it far enough in advance, she will be able to make plans with her own family or friends and have the extra gift of anticipation.

Today I will take time to rest and review my week.

Have I been willing to listen like a friend?

Have I followed through with any of my good intentions?

Have I been gentle with myself when I didn't follow through?

I walked along, tears brimming.
From nowhere she came, eyes bright and clear,
Helping me to unburden with her kindness, and I think...
How grateful I am for her thoughtfulness.

Now I can smile, my eyes bright and clear.
Approached by another fearful soul, eyes searching and scared,
I lead her, sharing my story, and I think,
How grateful she seemed to be for my thoughtfulness.

—Patty Casey

Today's Thoughtful Action Step/Love

Today I will let those close to me know
that I love them, knowing that life doesn't
always give us tomorrow.

Affirmation/Positive Words

When I hear toxic words polluting the airwaves, I will leave, change the channel, turn off the radio, or put down the telephone. Violent, negative, abusive words pollute my thoughts and influence my mood and actions.

As I become more aware of the negative and positive influences on my spirit, I no longer need to stay within hearing range of any words that take me away from my higher purpose.

Today I will take time to reflect on what the following thought means to me:

Everyone should know that you can't live in any other way than by cultivating the soul.

—Apuleius

When I take the time to be thoughtful, I can enjoy the closeness of friends and family, the beauty of nature and the love of God in a way not possible when I am preoccupied with yesterday or tomorrow.

December 8

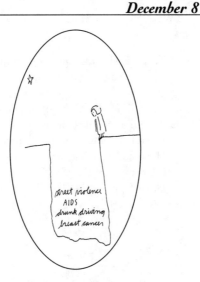

Today's Thoughtful Action
Step/Prayer

I will take quiet time today to pray for
the end of street violence, AIDS, drunk
driving and breast cancer. I will add any
other areas I feel strongly about and
make a note to do this on a regular basis.

**Today I will take time to rest and
review my week.**

Have I refused to be drawn into the
violence that pollutes life today?

Have I shared my pain with another?

Have I been willing to offer my time to
help others enjoy theirs?

Have I prayed for the end of suffering?

Ann Landers suggests that if someone says something rude, we should respond with "What did you say?" This gives the person an opportunity to rethink and rephrase their statement, perhaps being kinder the second time.

Today's Thoughtful Action
Step/Plan of Action

Today I will take some time to reflect on a plan of action I can follow which will improve my life and the lives of others. I will take the time to write down this plan and keep it where I will remain conscious of it each day, adding to it, changing it and making it my personal plan of action.

Affirmation/Loving Thoughts

Today I will imagine one person I
would like to help and spend a few
moments by sending loving thoughts
their way.

Today I will take time to reflect on
what the following thought means to me:

*When you touch a fellow human being
in love you are doing God's work.*

—Unknown

When I take the time to be thoughtful, I can get out of my own way. I can be aware of someone around me who could use some encouragement. I can give a warm smile or a comforting word.

Today's Thoughtful Action
Step/Treat People

Treat people as if they were what they
ought to be and you will help them
become what they are capable
of becoming.

—Goethe

In raising my children, as well as in all
my relationships with people, I have tried
to live by these words. It has brought me
wonderful results, not the least of which
is the love of my family and friends:

Today I will continue to treat people
as if they are what they ought to be!

—Fred Casson

Today's Thoughtful Action
Step/Good Impulses

In the Tao Te Ching we are told that the first impulse of the heart is always good. Often we stop ourselves from acting on our good impulses. We hold back with negative thoughts such as: "What will people think?" "It won't matter anyway." "He won't want to hear it." "It isn't appropriate."

Today I will take a risk and do something thoughtful. I will get beyond my self-consciousness and self-concern.

Affirmation/Awareness

Today I am developing my ability to be thoughtful by being more aware of my actions.

As more and more of us further develop our ability to be thoughtful, we will see that thoughtfulness has the power to heal the world.

Today I will take time to reflect on
what the following thought means to me:

*What we expect, believe and
picture, we usually get.*

—Ruth Ross

When I take the time to be thoughtful,
I can consider today's important question:
Am I aware of how I speak to myself?
Do I nurture myself or destroy my
own self-esteem?

. . . If we listen to the way that we speak
to ourselves when we make mistakes,
we may be able to hear whether or not
we are nurturing or destroying ourselves
and our self-esteem.

—Marsha Sinetar

Today's Thoughtful Action Step/Work

I will do my own work today as if it were a service to others. Indeed, it is!

Be good, sweet maid and let who can be clever.
Do noble things, not dream them all day long.
And so make life one long, sweet song.

— As told to Marie Stilkind
by her mother

**Today I will take time to rest and
review my week.**

Have I discovered the miracles of
thoughtfulness?

Thoughtful acts do not have to be overwhelming commitments of time, presence or money. Thoughtfulness can be integrated into busy lifestyles and expressed on a regular basis as part of one's regular daily routine. Over time we can develop a few simple thoughtful habits that can bring smiles and joy to others.

—Diana Smith

Today's Thoughtful Action
Step/Spirituality

As I go about my day I will be open to other thoughtful people who are following a spiritual path. I know if my intention is to find them, I will. I will spend more time in the energy of other like-minded individuals who wish to make the world a better place for all.

Affirmation/Awareness

Today I am increasing my awareness of all the ways in which I can be thoughtful.

Today I will take time to reflect on what the following thought means to me:

Today I know that God chooses the people to whom God wants me to be accessible to so that I might pass on God's love to them. They may or may not always be the person I might pick or it might not even be a convenient time for me. But I will trust God's direction and follow it.

—Sally Butler

When I take the time to be thoughtful, I can consider today's important questions:

Am I becoming a more thoughtful human being?

Am I becoming more compassionate to the suffering of others?

Am I discovering, one day at a time, the purpose of my life?

Am I in the flow of goodness and love?

Am I on the path of right thought and action?

Am I growing as a spiritual human being?

Am I doing things that make my heart sing?

Am I becoming more and more connected to everyone and everything in the universe?

Am I connected to a power greater than myself?

Today's Thoughtful Action
Step/Moving Forward

Thoughtfulness has the power to connect us with someone else. Thoughtfulness has the power to heal and the power to make us feel good and warm.

Thoughtfulness has the power to wipe away years of pain with a word, look or touch.

Thoughtfulness has the power to wipe away centuries of unthoughtfulness.

One act of thoughtfulness can bring peace.

Just thinking about doing one act of thoughtfulness has the power to open our heart and fill it with joy.

Today I am using the power of thoughtfulness to move forward in my life to open to all the possibilities it offers.

Affirmation/Miracles

Today I KNOW that thoughtfulness has a domino effect.

My thoughtfulness helps me to help someone else to help someone else to help someone else until . . . God bless us all!

God bless us all!

Today I will take time to rest and review the year!

It is time to give myself a pat on the back if one is due, and to see how my thoughtfulness contributes to the greater good.

It is time to celebrate the positive changes in the people around me.

It is time to let myself feel good about my connection to the growing number of people who are helping to change the world!

Today is just one day before the start of the next year. After I take this time to rest, I am willing to recommit myself to continue taking the _Time for Thoughtfulness_.

MAY THIS NEW YEAR BRING US ALL
PEACE AND LOVE AND FREEDOM.
MAY WE ALL CONTINUE OUR
POSITIVE INTENTIONS TO MAKE A
DIFFERENCE IN THE WORLD!
A VERY HAPPY NEW YEAR
TO EVERYONE! I LOVE YOU ALL!

Other Books by Ruth Fishel & Health Communications, Inc.®

Time for Joy
Daily Affirmations
Ruth Fishel takes you through a calendar year with joyful quotations, thoughts, and healing, energizing affirmations.
Code 4826 . . . . $6.95

The Journey Within
A Spiritual Path to Recovery
A book leading you from dysfunction to the place within where your wounded being can grow healthy and strong, the place where miracles happen.
Code 4826 . . . . $8.95

Learning to Live in the Now
6-Week Personal Plan to Recovery
Enjoy today without worrying about the future or regretting the past. There is only this moment. Savor it with this loving book.
Code 4621 . . . . $8.95

5 Minutes for World Peace . . . Forever
A 90-Day Affirmation Plan for Personal and World Peace
A five-minute-a-day, 90-day action plan for bringing peace to you and those around you.
Code 1690 . . . . $4.95

For Visa or MasterCard orders call: 1-800-441-5569.
Mention response code HCI. Prices do not include S&H.

For up-to-date information on Ruth Fishel's retreats, advances, workshops, conferences and tapes, or to be on her mailing list, contact her at:

Spirithaven
17 Pond Meadow Drive
Marstons Mills, MA 02648
(508) 420-5301
E-mail: *spirithaven@spirithaven.com*

Ruth Fishel's Audiotapes

The following tapes are available for purchase from Health Communications, Inc.

You Cannot Meditate Wrong!!! $8.95

Time for Joy..$9.95

These tapes are available from Ruth Fishel

Transforming Your Past into Presents: Finding Your Own Special Gifts....................................... $9.00

Guided Exercises for Deepening Your Meditation Experience $9.00

The Journey Within $9.00

Discovering Your Source of Peace with the Powerful Tool of Noting..$9.00